Eleven Plus Exam Group

Eleven Plus
Practice Paper

Non-Verbal Reasoning

Paper NVR 1
Dual Format
Standard and Multiple choice

60 Questions to be completed in 50 minutes

Name: _____

Date: _____

Score: _____

© Eleven Plus Exam Group 2010

Section A

In the questions below you will find five boxes on the left-hand side of the page. These boxes are arranged in order.

One of the boxes has been left empty.

You must choose one of the boxes from the right hand side that will take the place of the empty box and circle the correct letter below it, or mark the appropriate box on the multiple choice answer sheet.

Example:

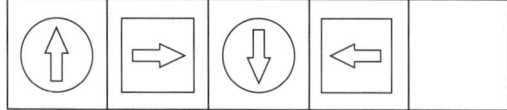 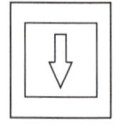  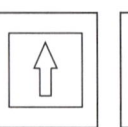 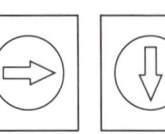

a b c d e

Answer: b.

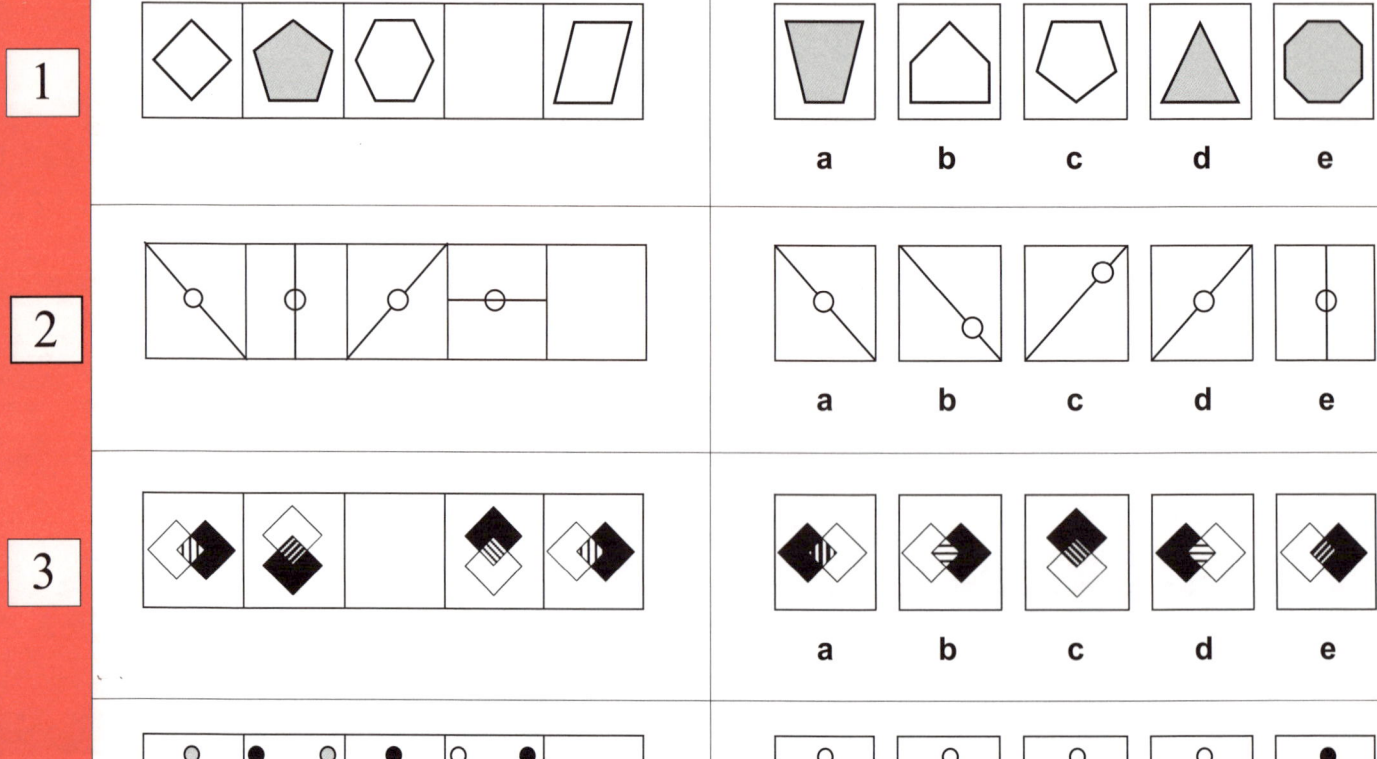

MOVE ON TO THE NEXT PAGE

© Eleven Plus Exam Group 2010

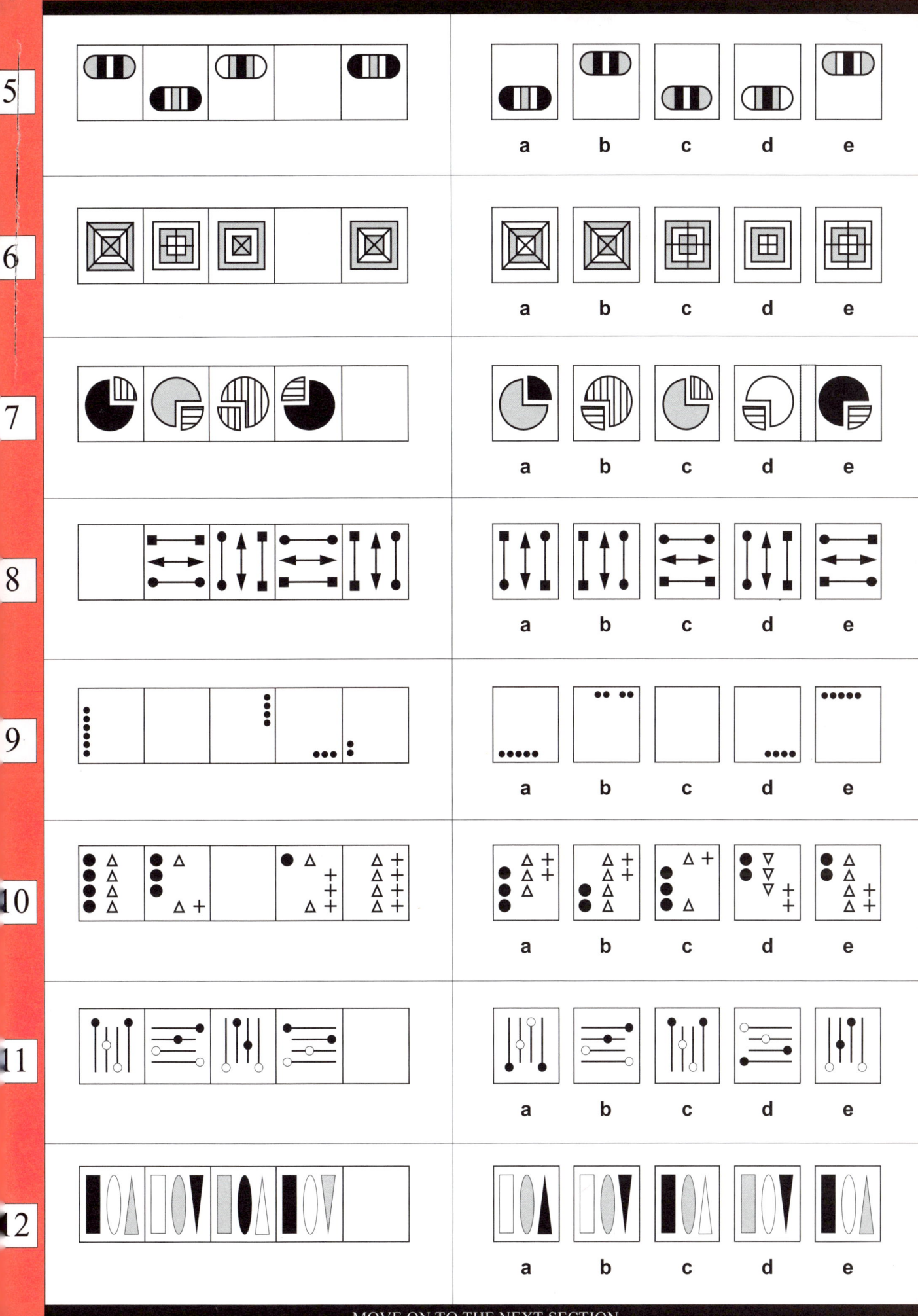

Section B

In the questions below there are two shapes on the left-hand side of the page. These shapes are separated by an arrow. Look carefully and try to decide how the pair are related.

After this pair there is a third shape, followed by an arrow, and then five more shapes.
You must decide which of the group of five shapes goes with the **third shape** to make a pair, like the pair on the left of the page.

Circle the letter under the shape, or mark the appropriate box on the multiple choice answer sheet.

Example

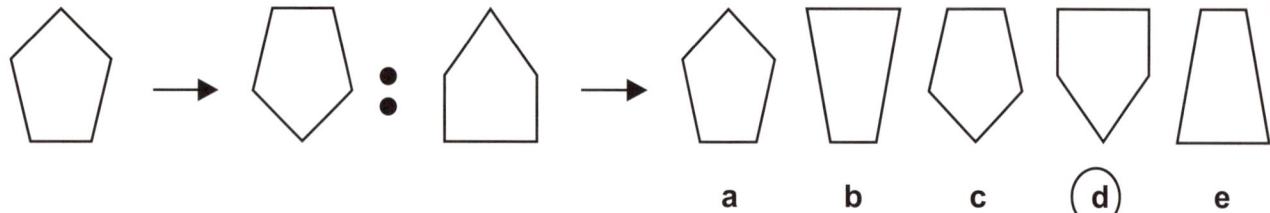

Answer: d

1.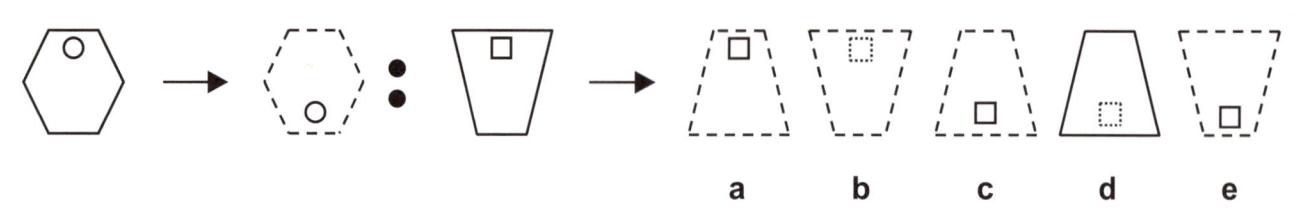

2.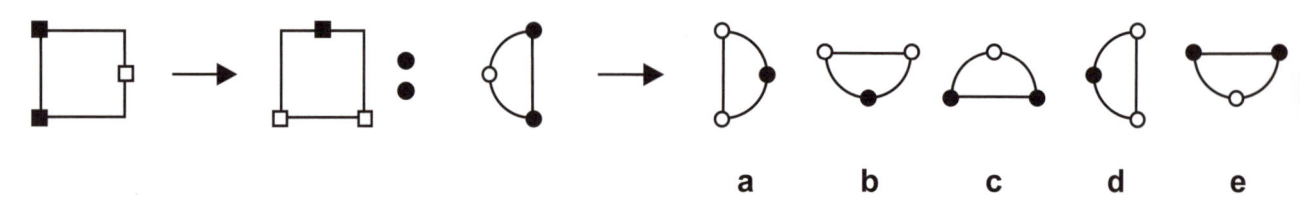

MOVE ON TO THE NEXT PAGE

3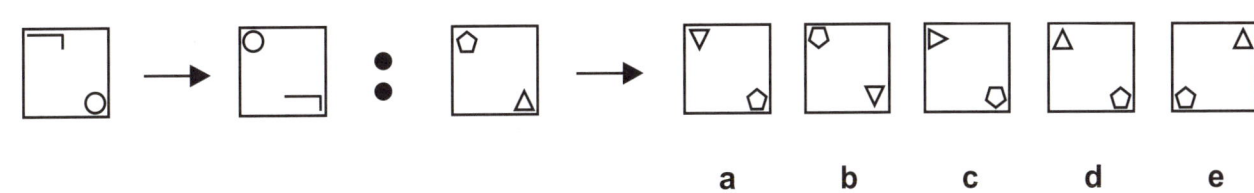

4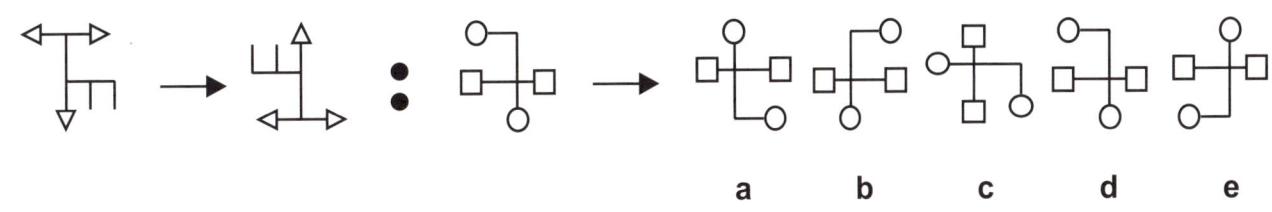

5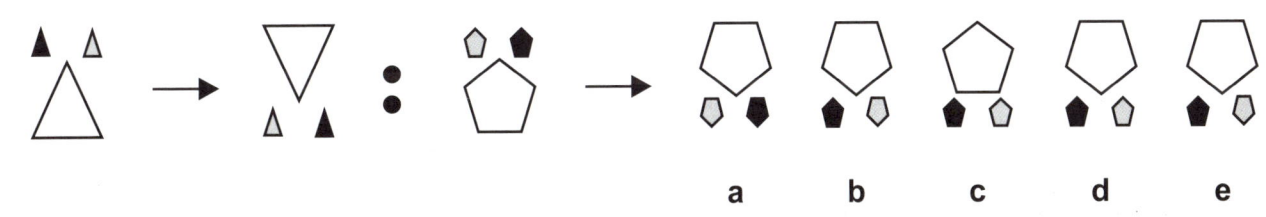

6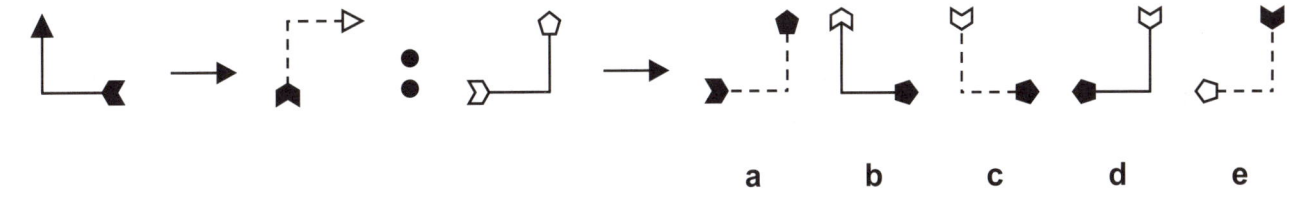

7

8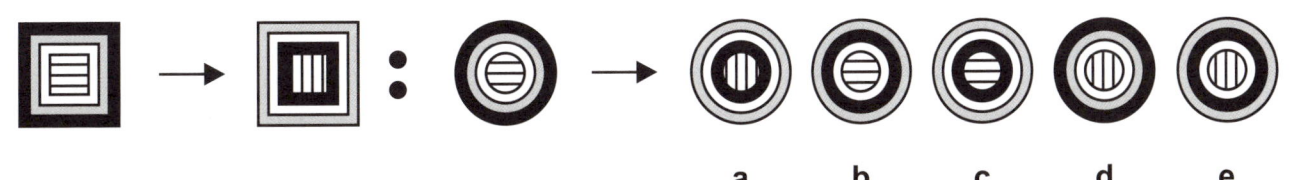

MOVE ON TO THE NEXT PAGE

© Eleven Plus Exam Group 2010

9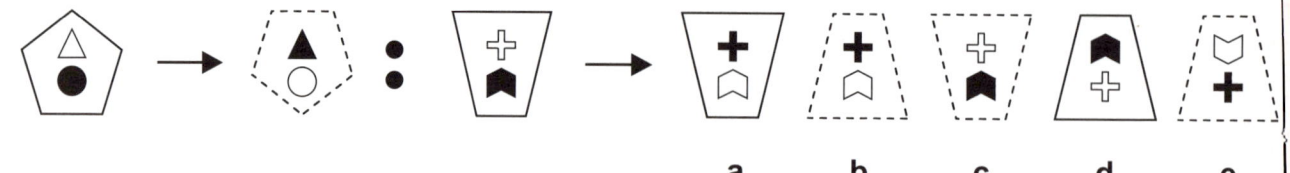

10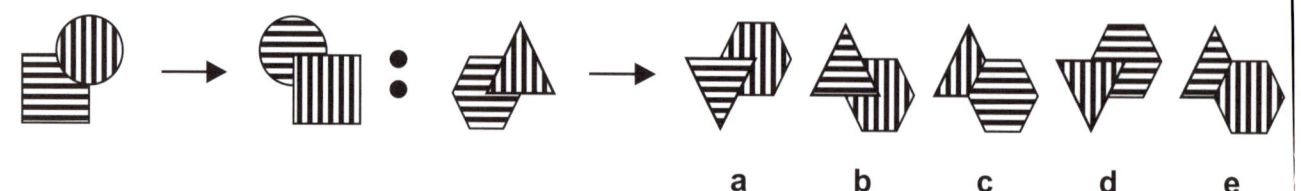

11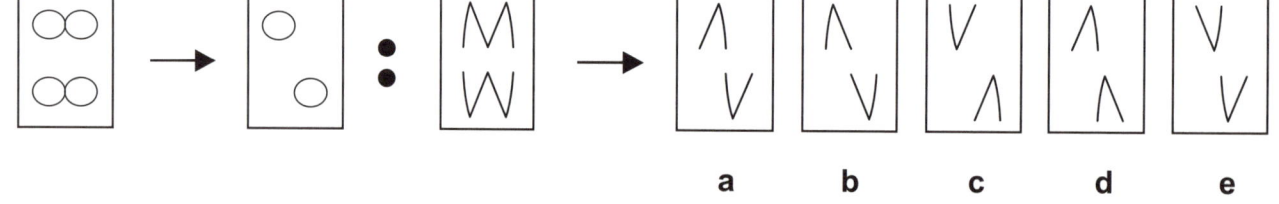

12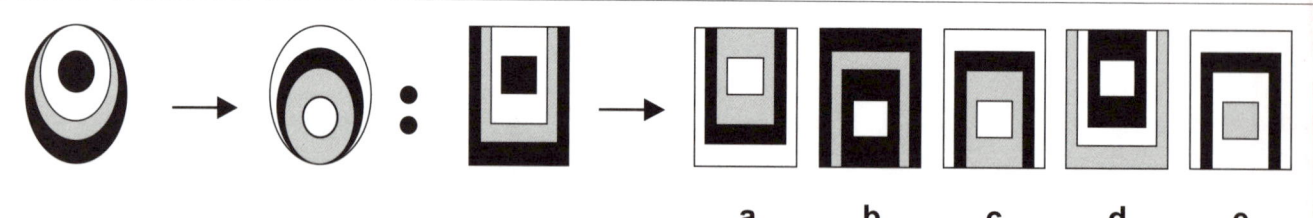

MOVE ON TO THE NEXT SECTION

Section C

To answer the following questions you will need to work out a code. On the left-hand side of the page there are some shapes and their codes. You must work out how the letter codes go with the shapes.

Using this information you must choose one of the codes from the right hand side that best describes the shape without a code. Circle the correct letter below it, or mark the appropriate box on the multiple choice answer sheet.

Example 1

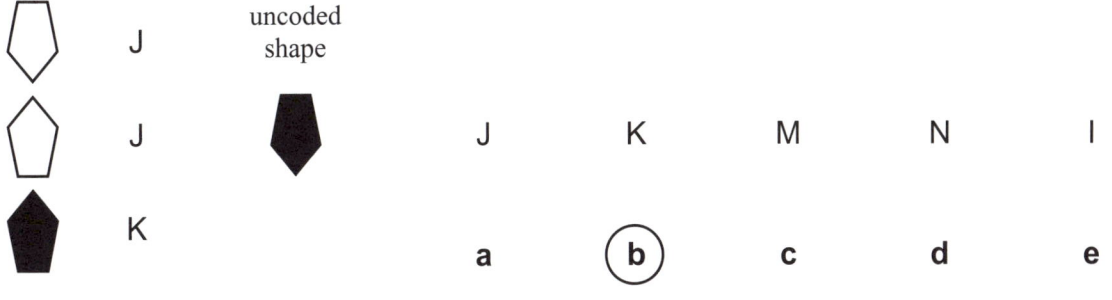

J	K	M	N	I
a	(b)	c	d	e

Answer: **b**

Two of the shapes have the code letter J. What makes these similar is that they are not shaded. The shaded shape has the code letter K. Therefore the un-coded shape must have the code letter K as it is shaded and the answer is **b**.

Example 2

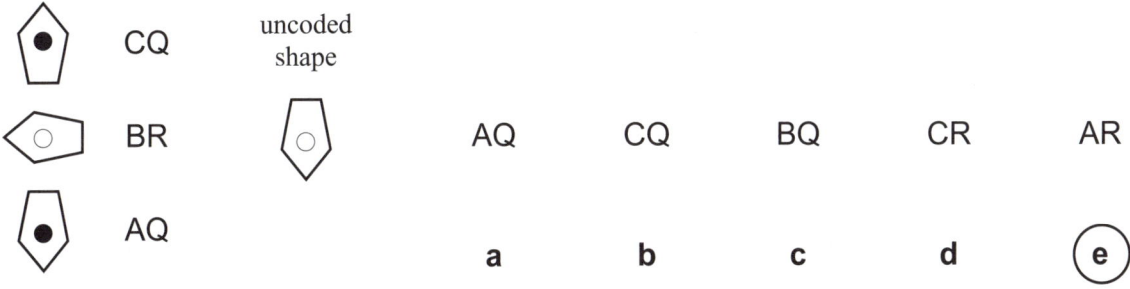

AQ	CQ	BQ	CR	AR
a	b	c	d	(e)

Answer: e

In this example each shape has two code letters. The first letter of each code refers to one aspect of the shape. Each shape has a different letter **A**, **B**, and **C**. What is different about each of the shapes? They are each turned in a different direction. The uncoded shape points in the same direction as **A**, so its code letter must be **A**.

The second code letter refers to another aspect of the shape. Two of the shapes have the code **Q**. What is the same in the shapes? They both have black circles, whereas the shape with the code **R** has a white circle. The uncoded shape has a white circle, and therefore the second code letter must be **R**.

Now we can tell that the code for the uncoded shape must be **AR**.

1

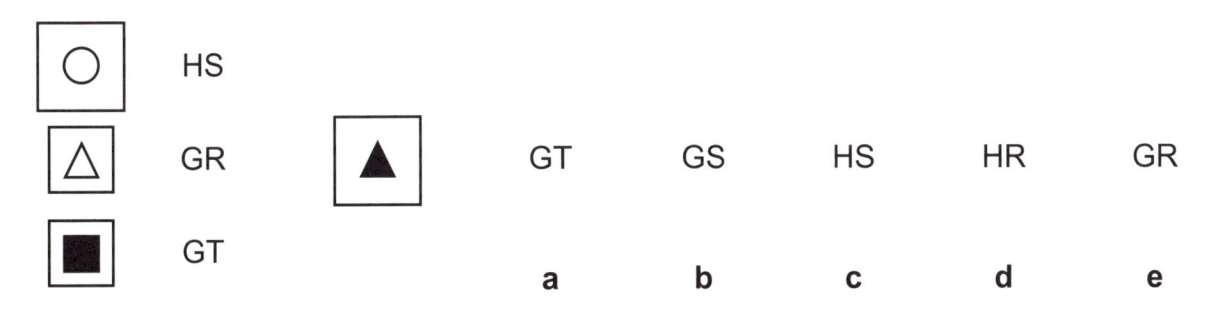

GT	GS	HS	HR	GR
a	b	c	d	e

MOVE ON TO THE NEXT PAGE

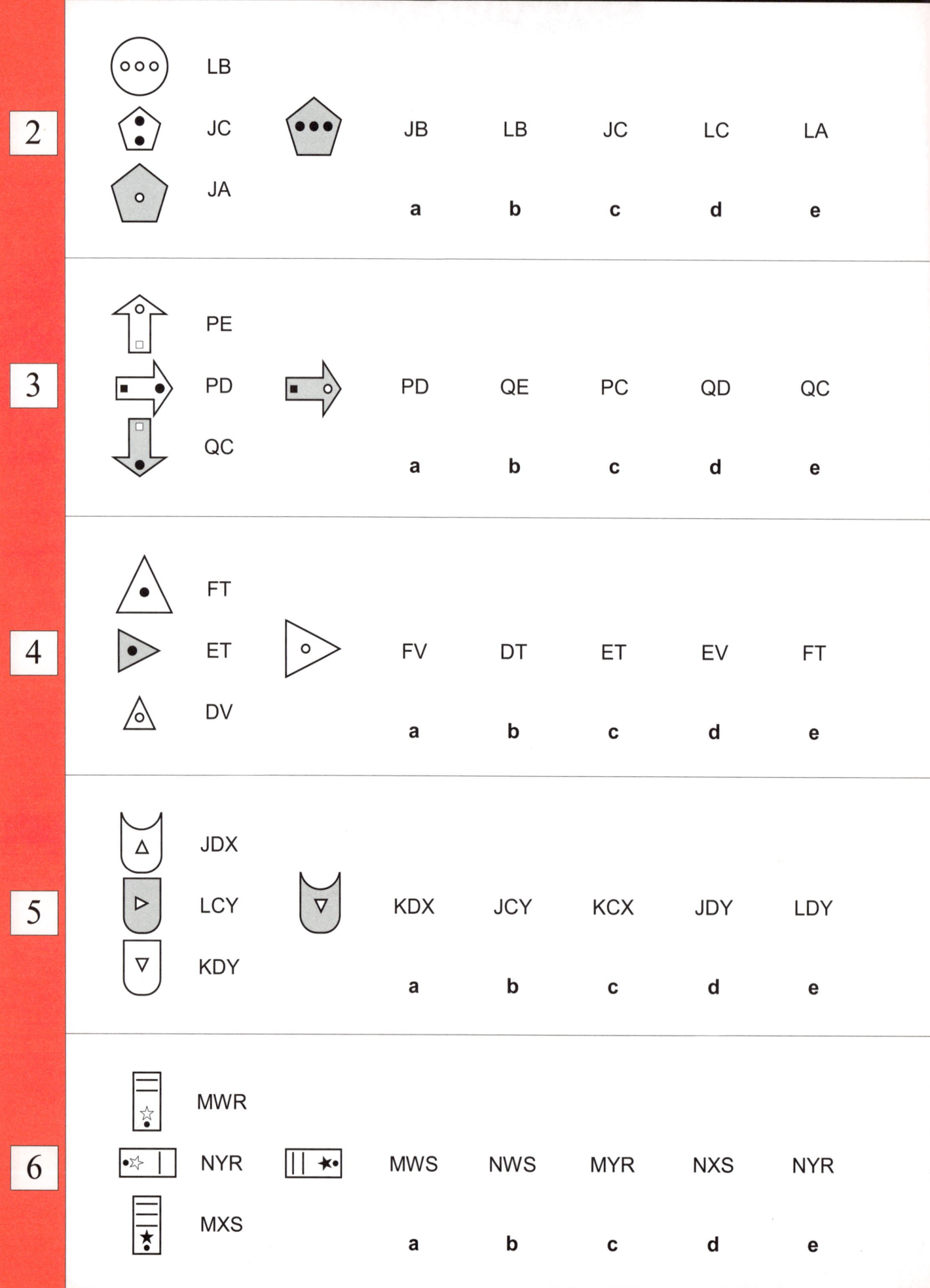

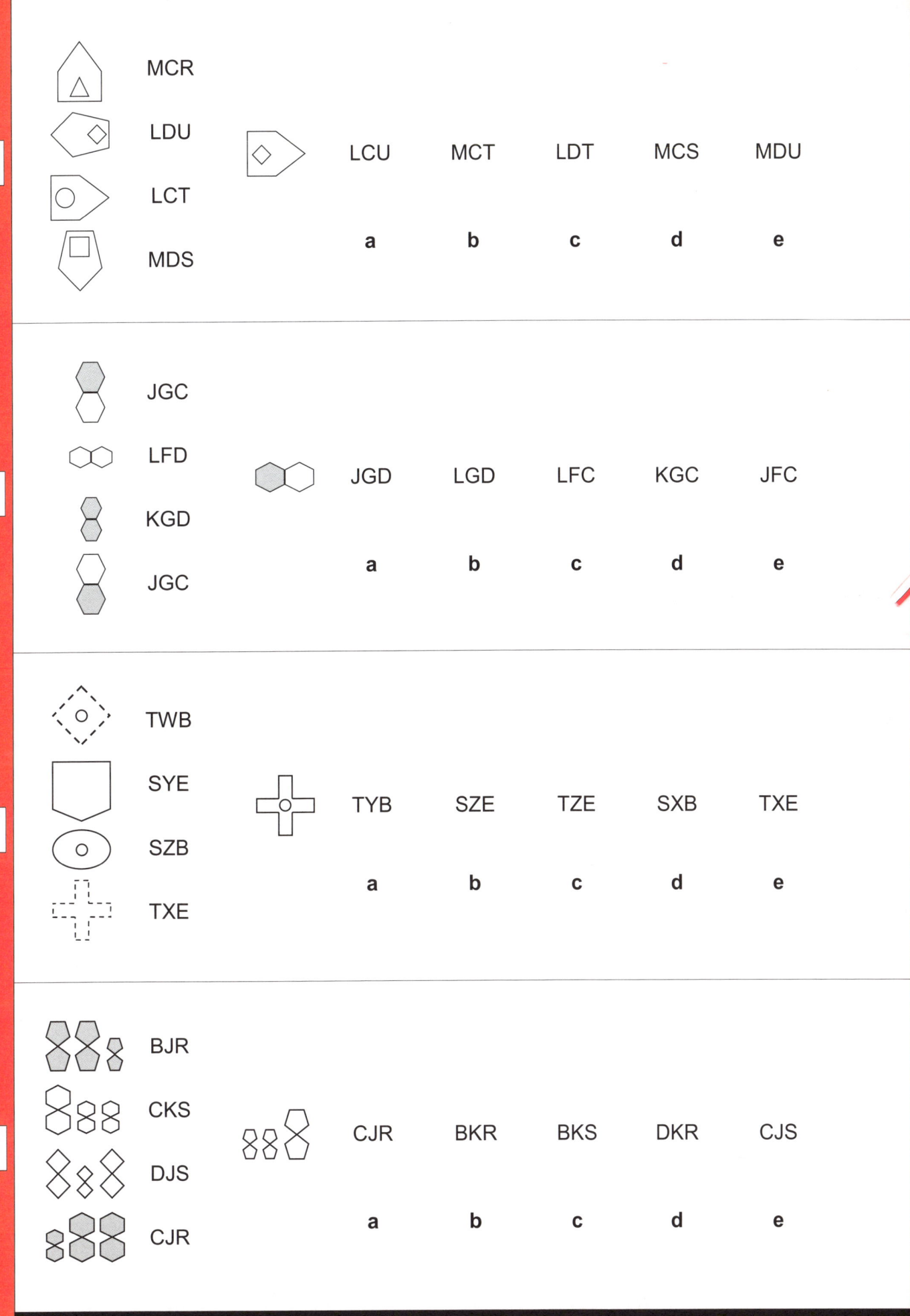

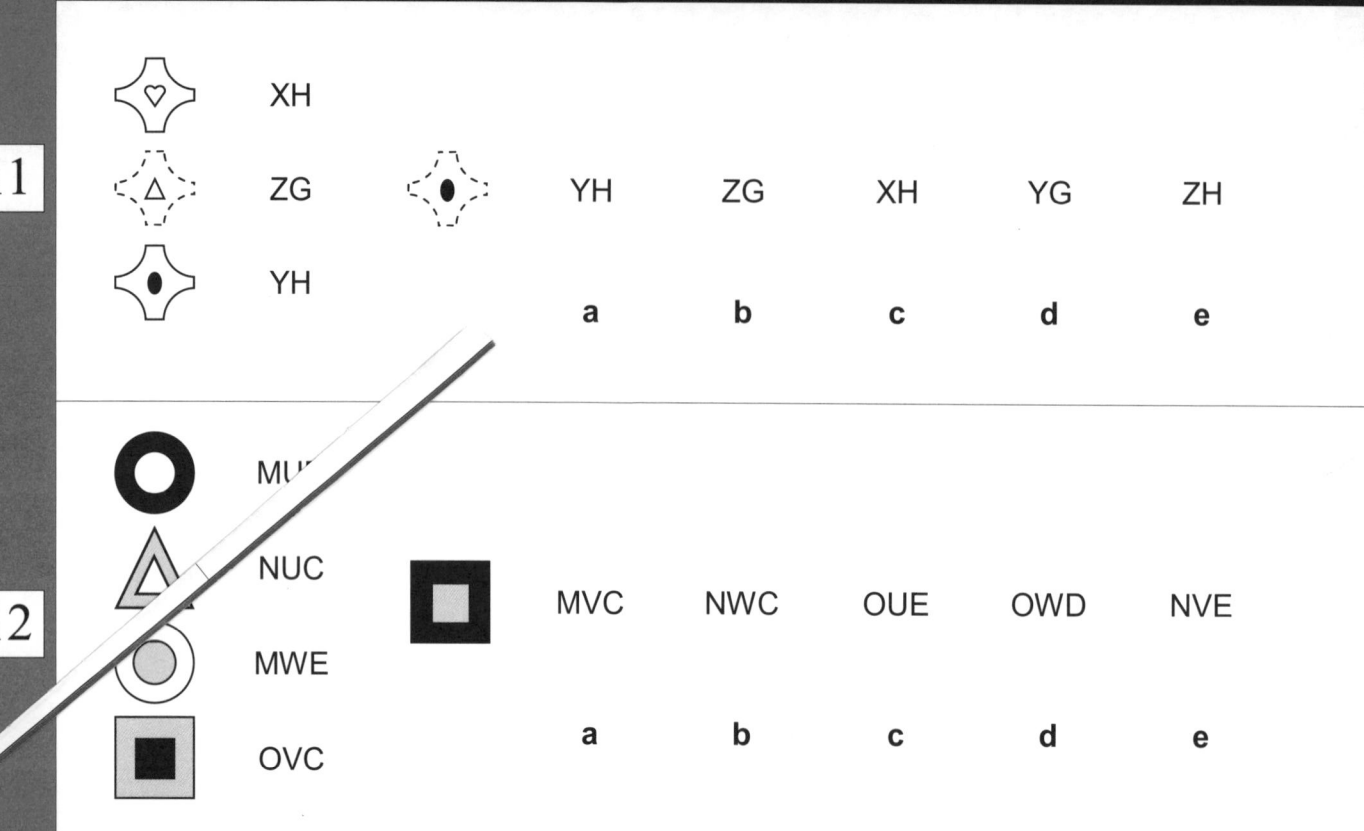

Section D

In the following questions there are two shapes on the left-hand side that are similar in some way. On the right-hand side there are five other shapes.

You must decide which **one** of the five shapes is most like the pair on the left side of the page. Circle the letter under the shape, or mark the appropriate box on the multiple choice answer sheet.

Example

a b c d (e)

Answer: e

1

a b c d e

2

a b c d e

3

a b c d e

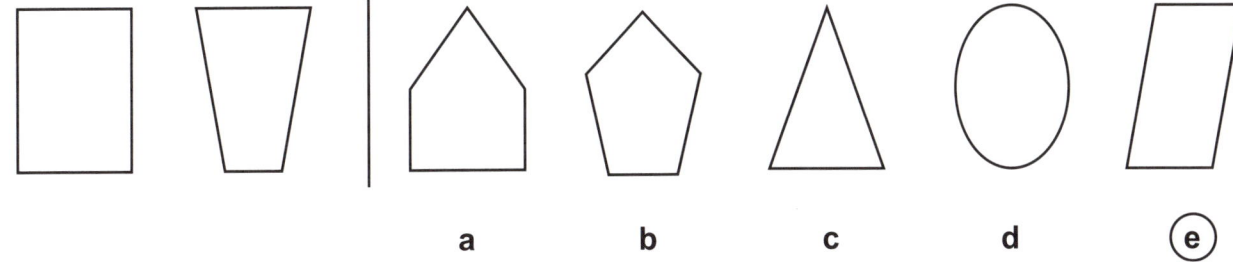

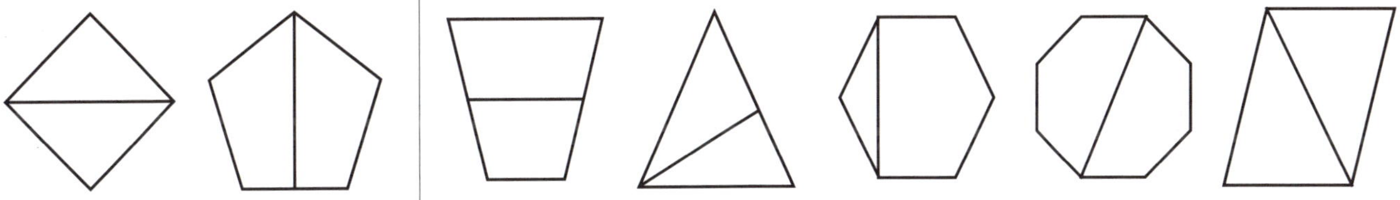

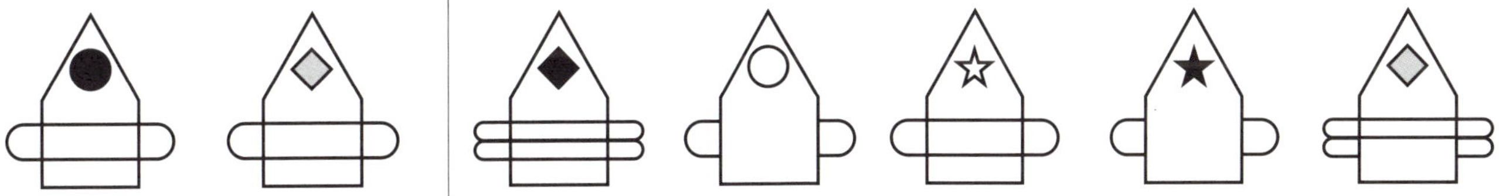

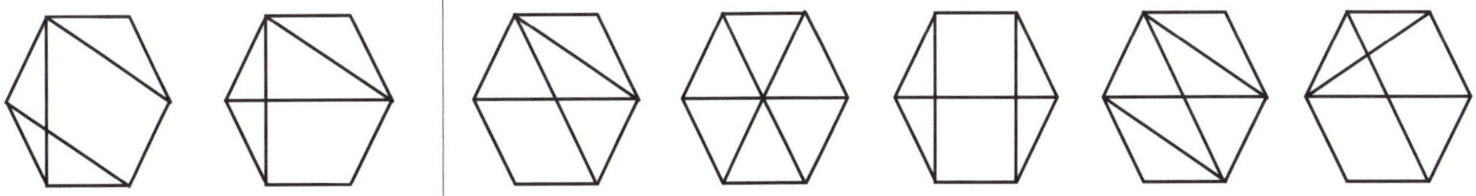

MOVE ON TO THE NEXT PAGE

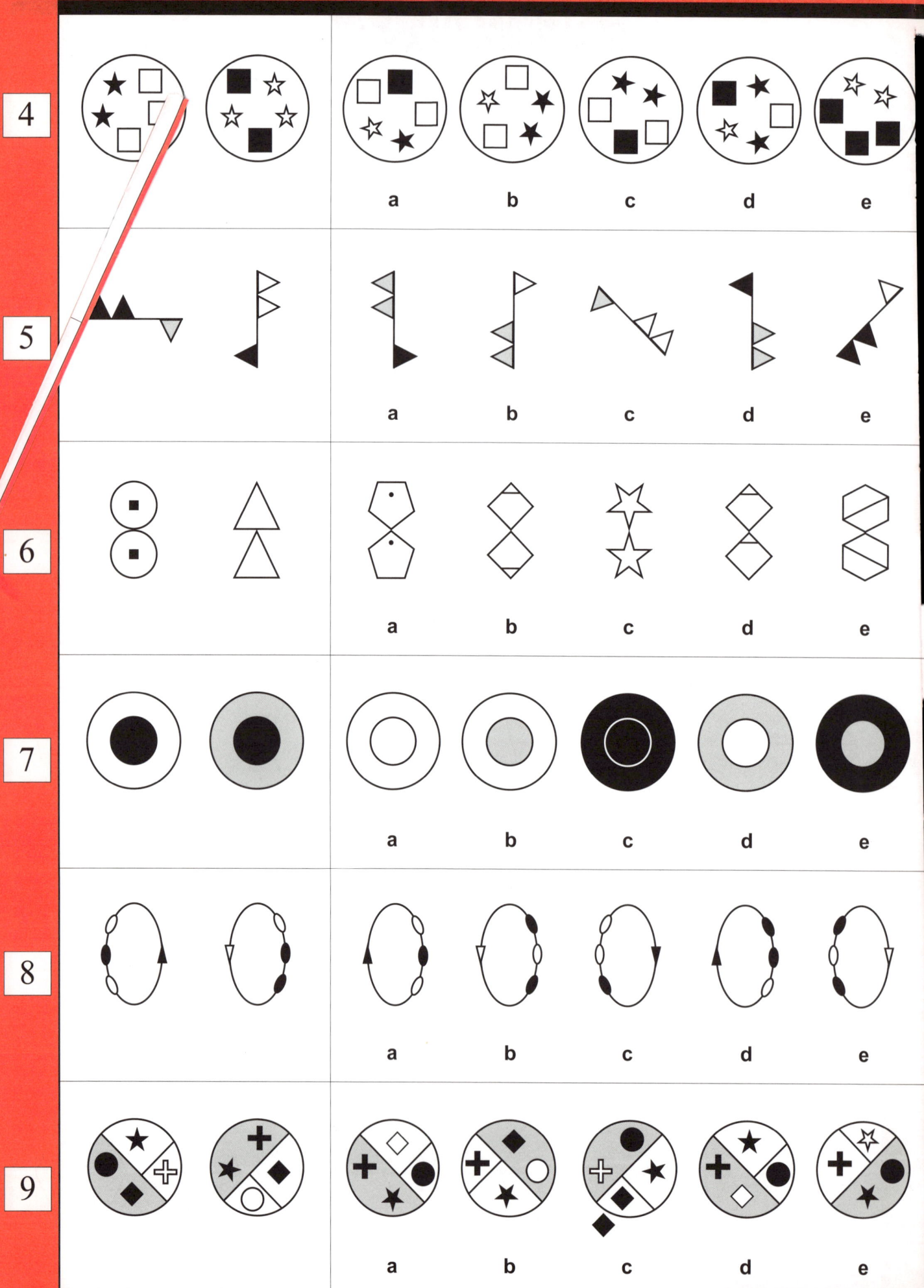

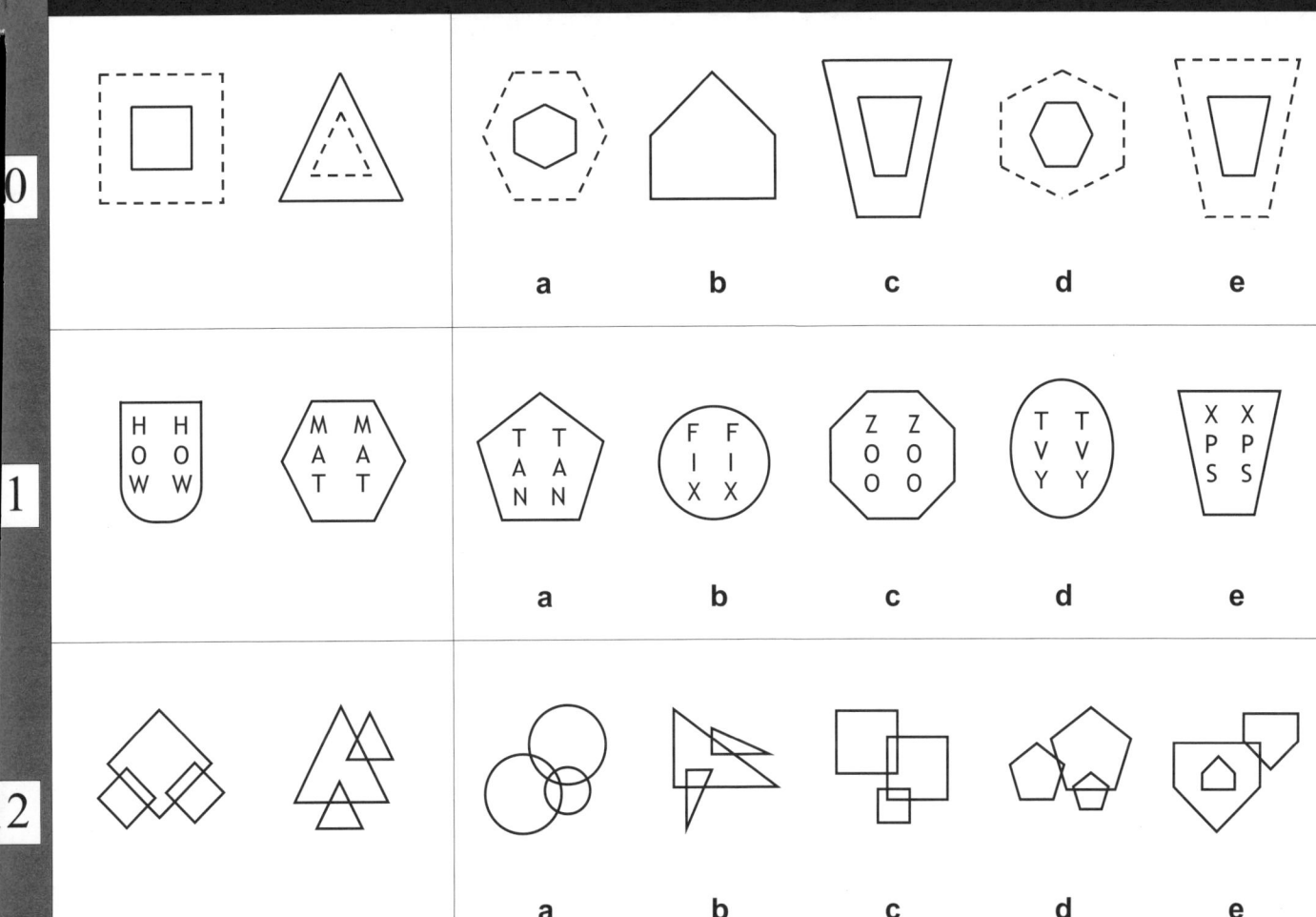

Section E

In the following questions there is a large square made up of smaller ones.
One of the smaller squares has been left blank.

You must choose one of the boxes from the right hand side that will take the place of the empty box and complete the pattern. Circle the letter below it, or mark the appropriate box on the multiple choice answer sheet.

Example

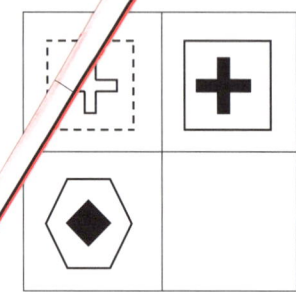 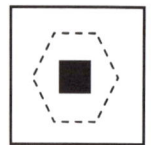 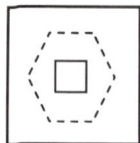 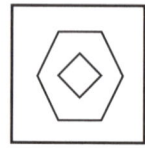  

                                            a   b   c   e

Answer: d

1

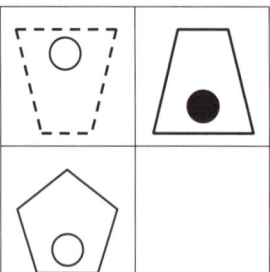 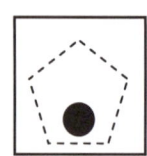   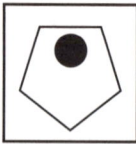 

                                            a   b   c   d   e

2

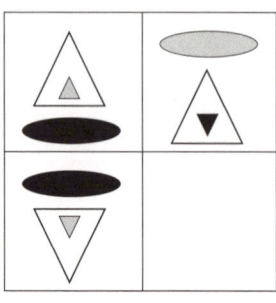 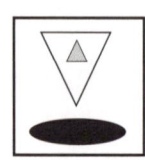 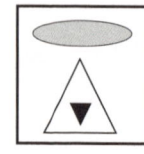 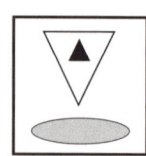 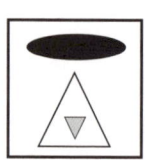 

                                            a   b   c   d   e

MOVE ON TO THE NEXT PAGE

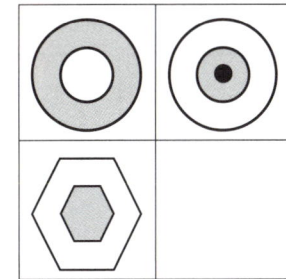 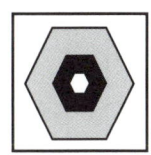 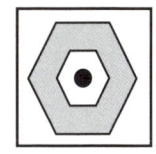 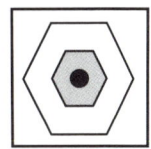 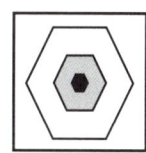 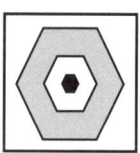

a b c d e

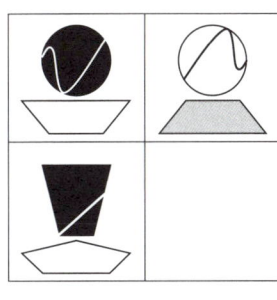  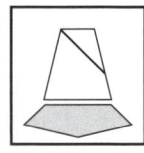 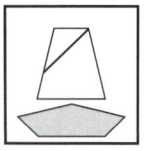 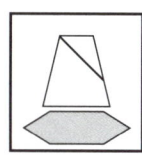 

a b c d e

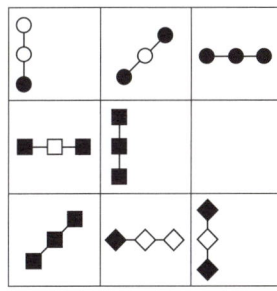  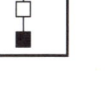 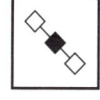

a b c d e

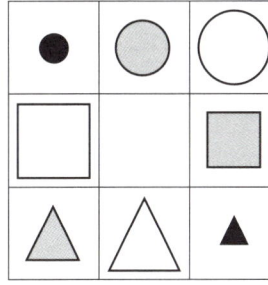    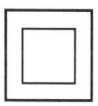 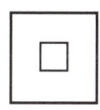 

a b c d e

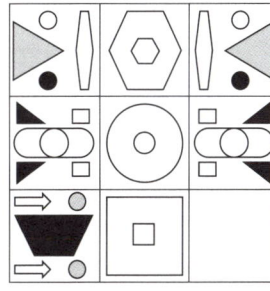  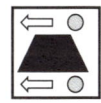 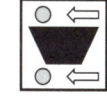  

a b c d e

MOVE ON TO THE NEXT PAGE

© Eleven Plus Exam Group 2010

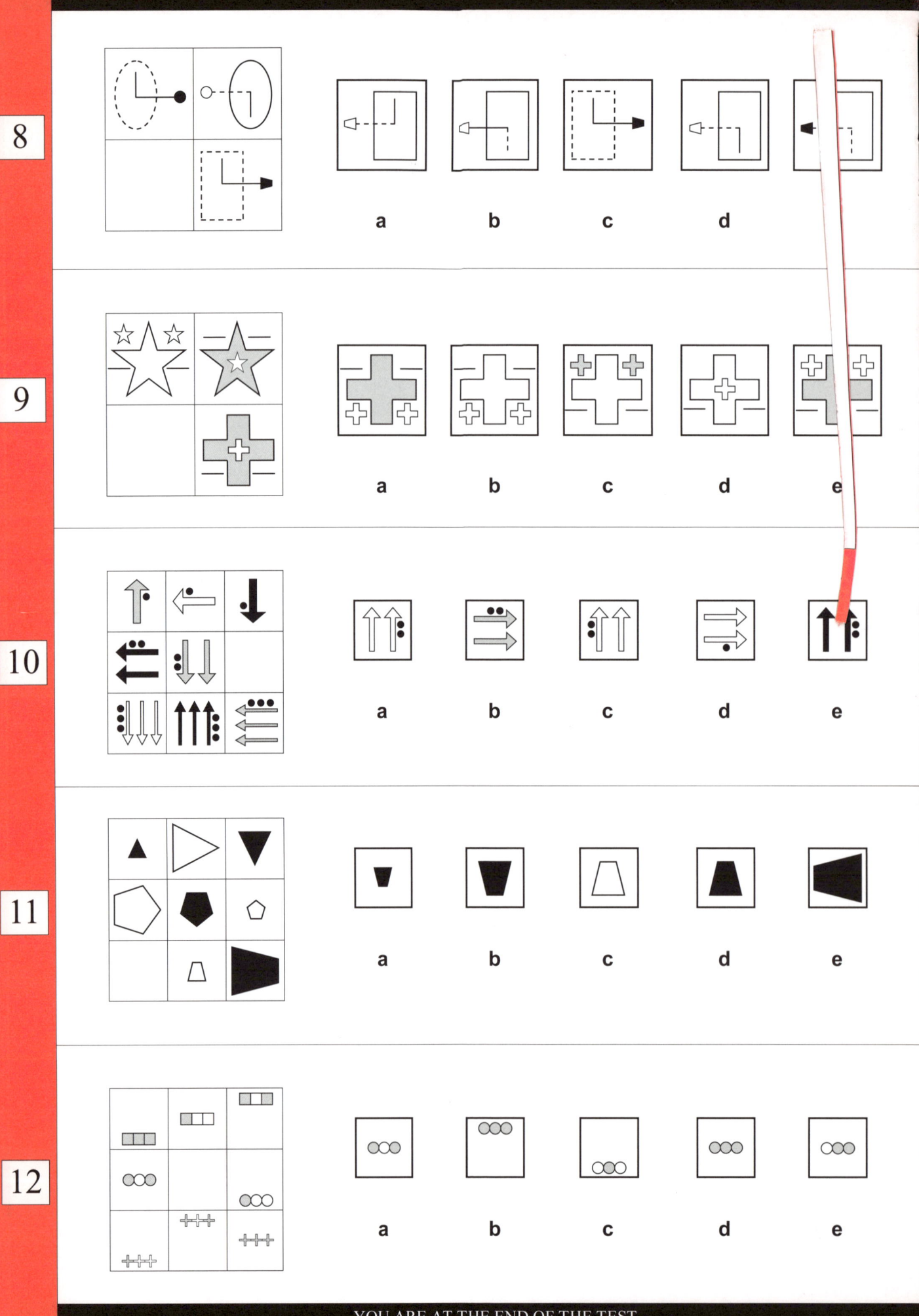

Eleven Plus Exam Group

Eleven Plus
Practice Paper

Non-Verbal Reasoning

Paper NVR 4

Dual Format
Standard and Multiple choice

60 Questions to be completed in 50 minutes

Name: _____

Date: _____

Score: _____

© Eleven Plus Exam Group 2010

Section A

In each of the following questions you will find five figures.

You must find the one figure from the five that is **most unlike** the rest.

Circle the correct letter below, or mark the appropriate box on the multiple choice answer sheet.

Example:

 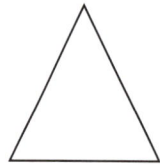 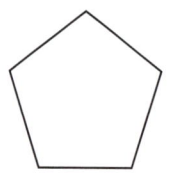 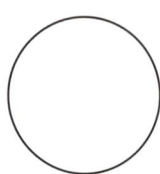 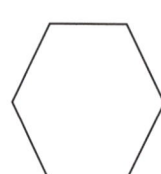

a   b   c   d   e

Answer: d

1.

a   b   c   d   e

2.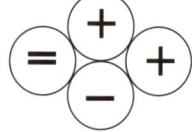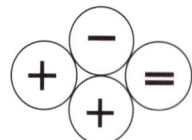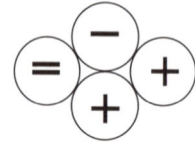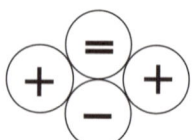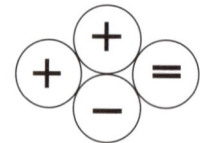

a   b   c   d   e

3.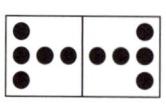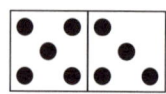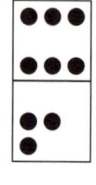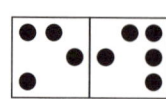

a   b   c   d   e

MOVE ON TO THE NEXT PAGE

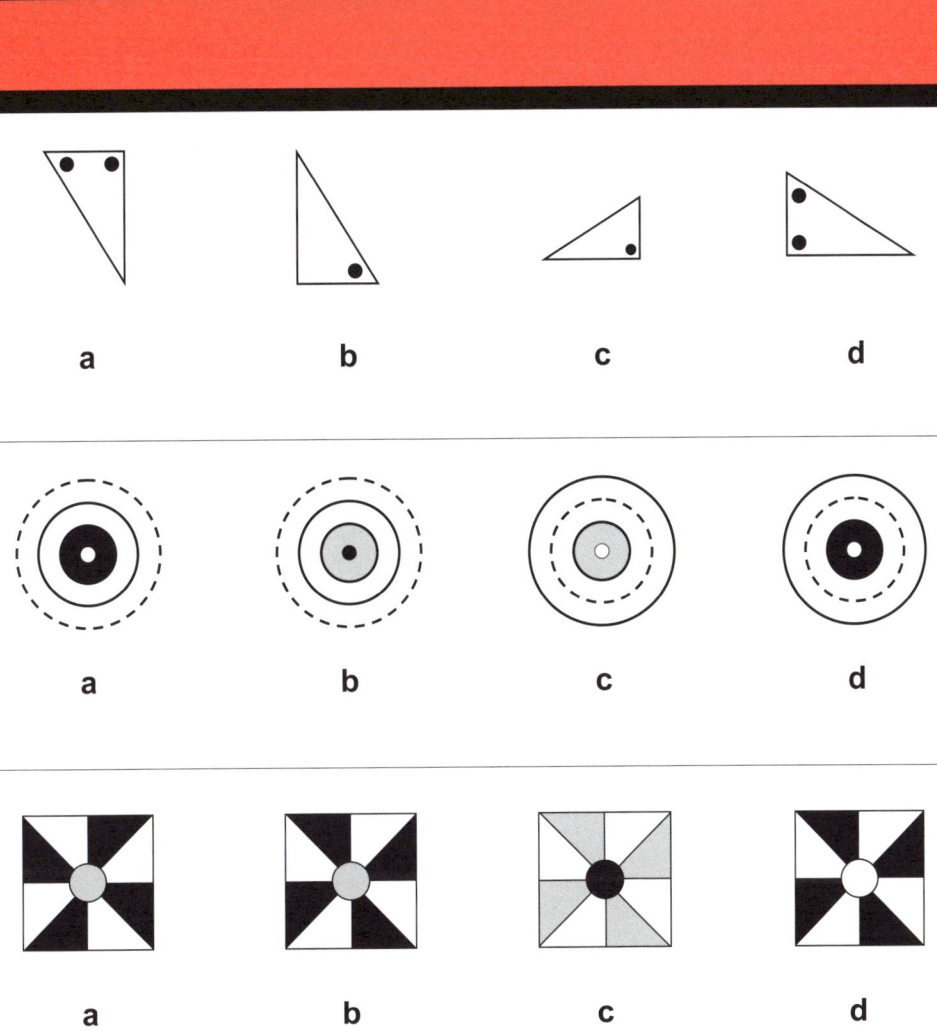

MOVE ON TO THE NEXT SECTION

Section B

To answer the following questions you will need to work out a code. In the boxes to the left of the page are shapes and code letters. The top letter in each box refers to one aspect of the shape, the bottom letter goes with another. You need to decide how the letters and shapes go together.

Now look at the shape on the right hand side of the page. You must choose one of the pairs of code letters to fill the empty spaces and circle the letter below it, or mark the appropriate box on the multiple choice answer sheet.

Example 1:

  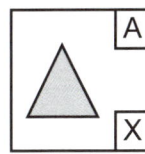 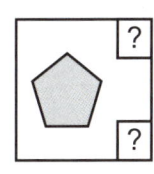 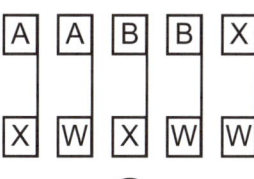

a   b   (c)   d   e

Answer: c

On the top row the code letter **A** appears twice. What is similar about these two shapes? They are both triangles. The code letter **W** appears twice below the shapes. What is similar about these shapes? They are both unshaded. Looking at the mystery shape we can see that it is a pentagon, which means that the first code letter should be **B.** It is also shaded, which means that the second code letter should be **X**. Therefore the answer is c. **BX**

Example 2:

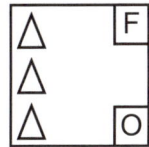 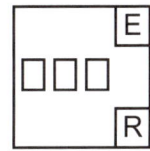  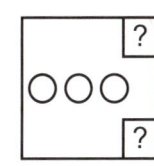 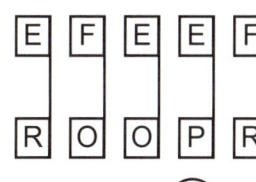

a   b   c   (d)   e

Answer: d

On the top row the code letter **F** appears twice. What is similar about these two shapes? They are both vertical. The code letter **P** appears only once below the shapes. All three code letters are different. What is different about all three shapes? They are formed from different shapes. Looking at the mystery box we can see the shape is horizontal, which means that the first code letter must be **E.** Its shape is a circle, and so the second code letter must be **P.** Therefore the answer is d. **EP**

---

1 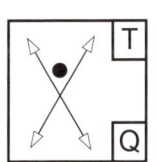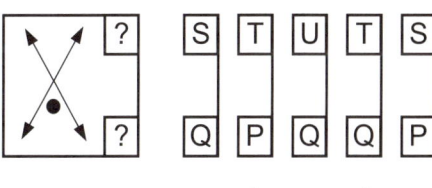

a   b   c   d   e

2 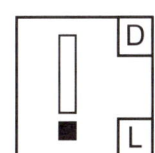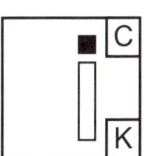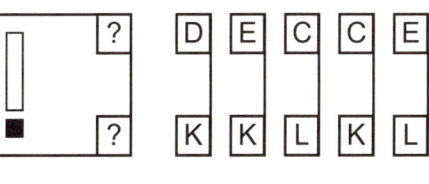

a   b   c   d   e

MOVE ON TO THE NEXT PAGE

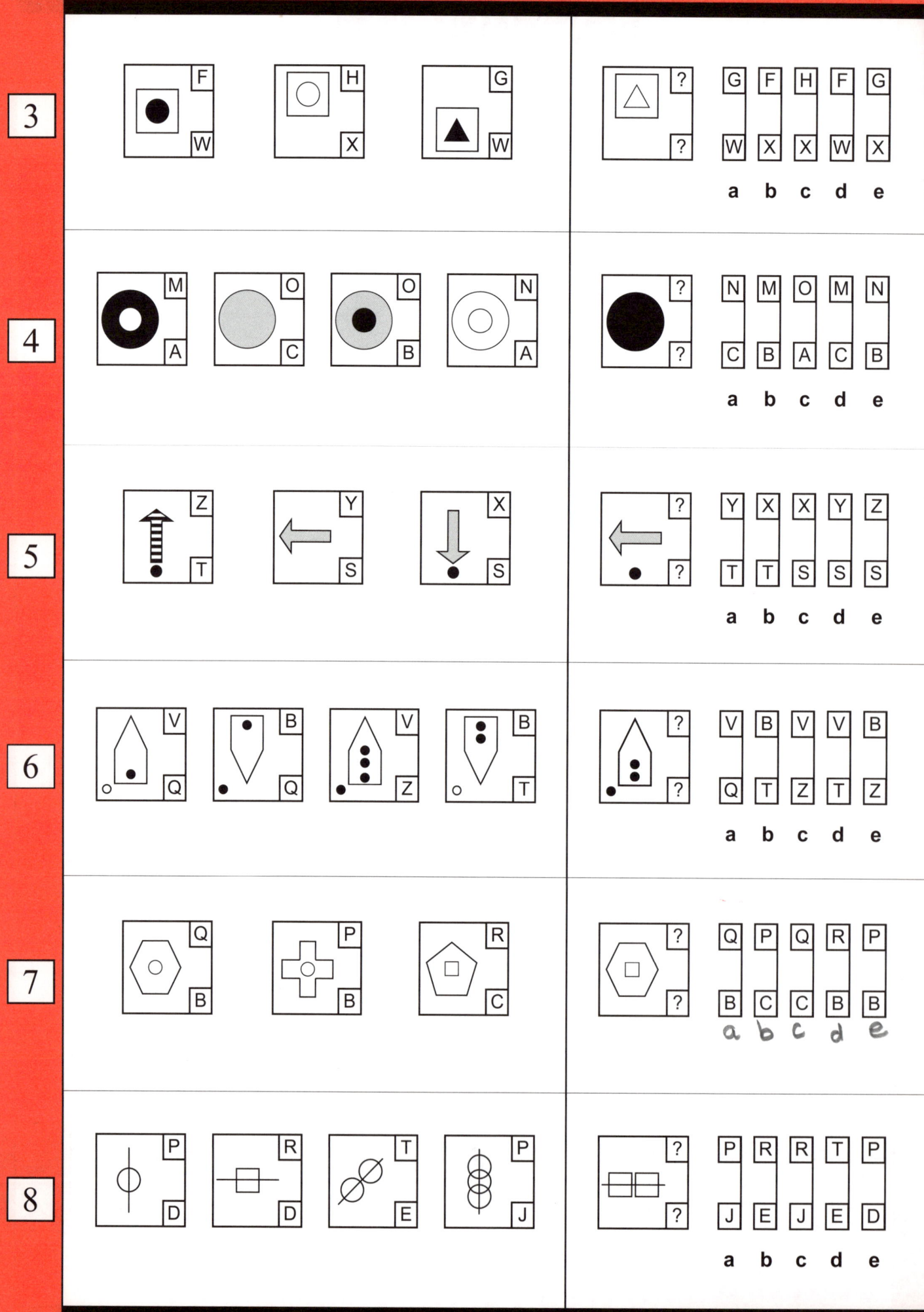

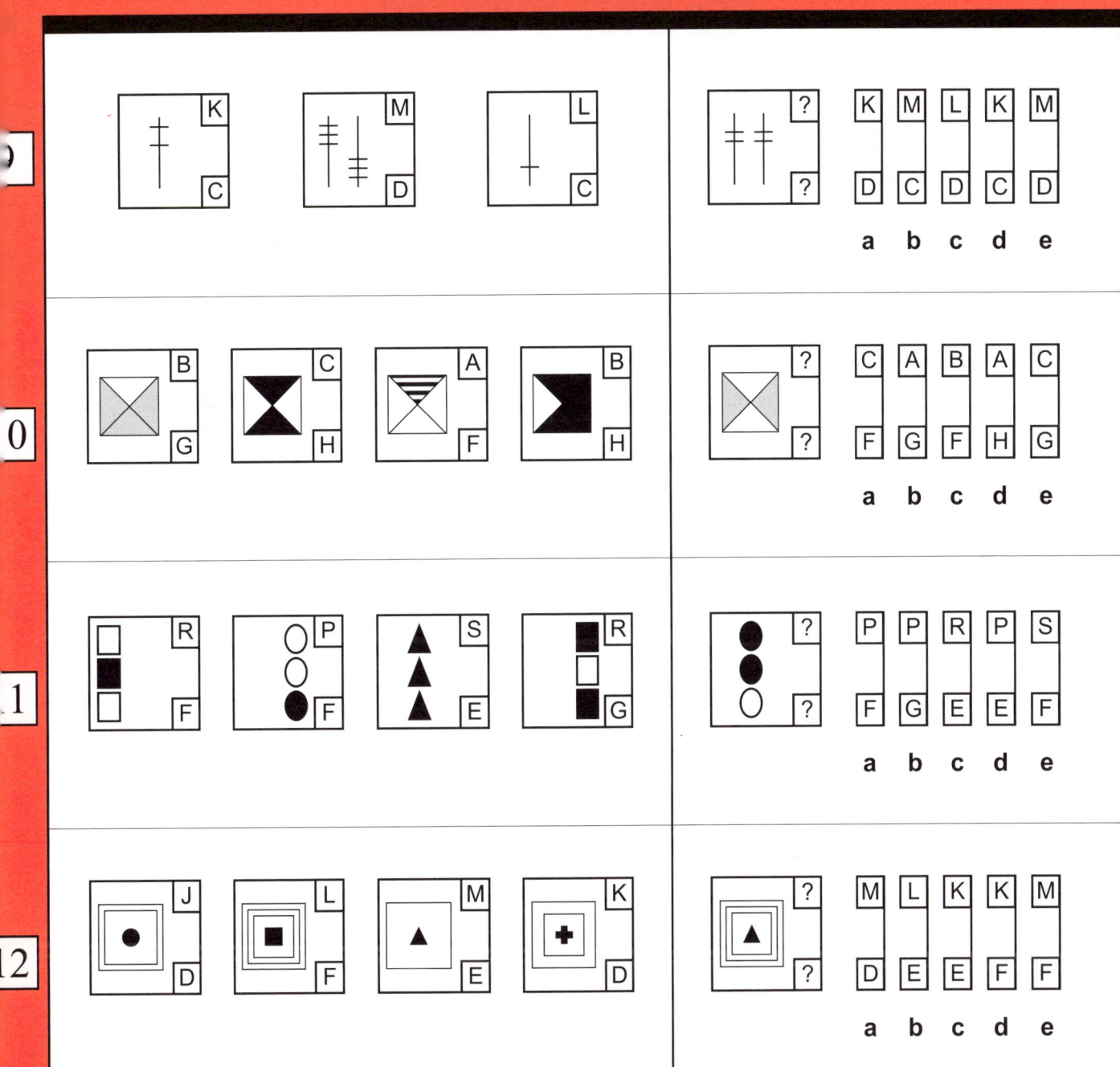

Section C

In the questions below there are two shapes on the left-hand side of the page. These shapes are separated by an arrow. Look carefully and try to decide how the pair are related.

After this pair there is a third shape, followed by an arrow, and then five more shapes.
You must decide which of the group of five shapes goes with the **third shape** to make a pair, like the pair on the left of the page.

Circle the letter under the shape, or mark the appropriate box on the multiple choice answer sheet.

Example

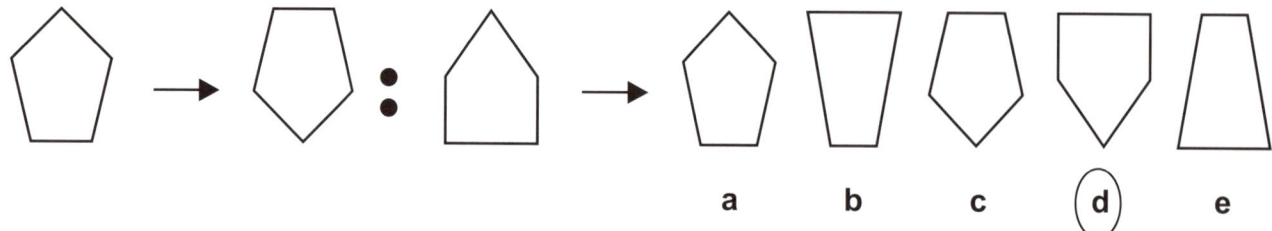

Answer: d

1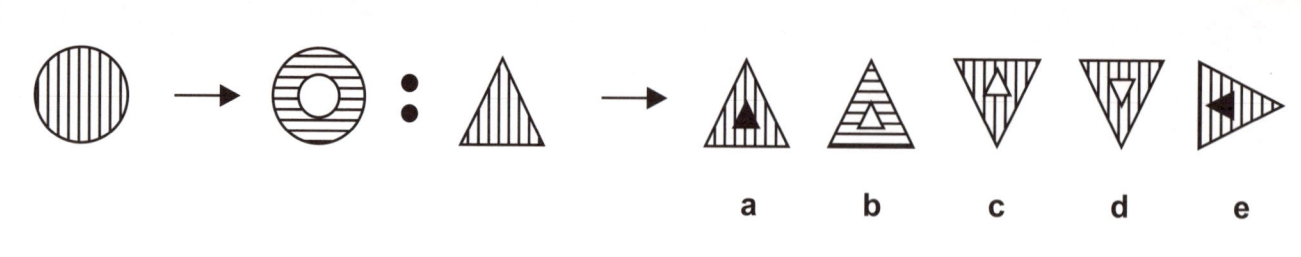

2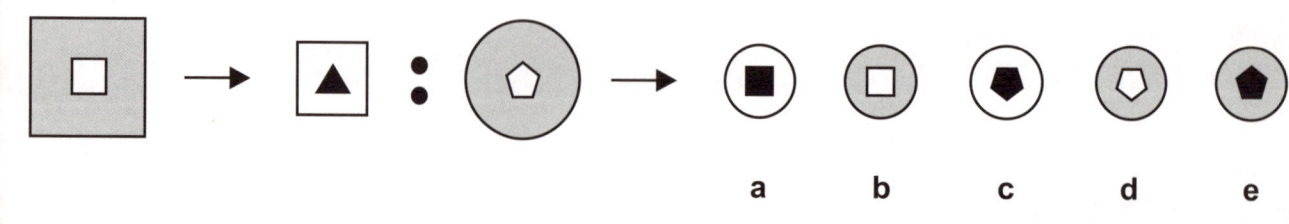

MOVE ON TO THE NEXT PAGE

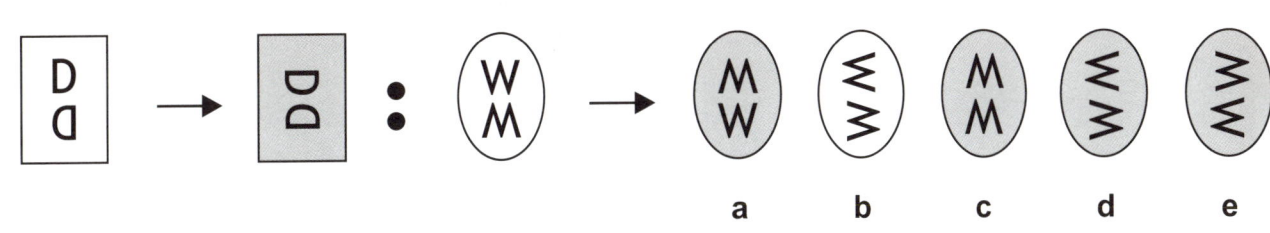
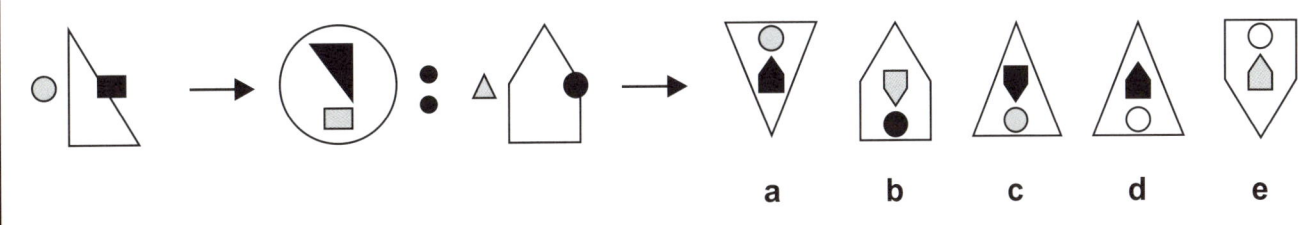
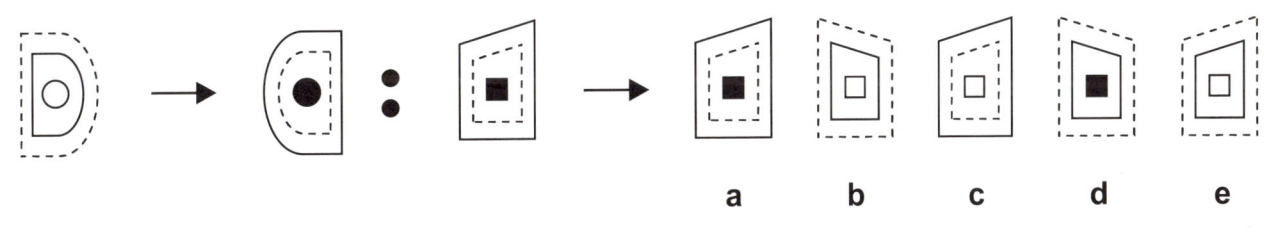
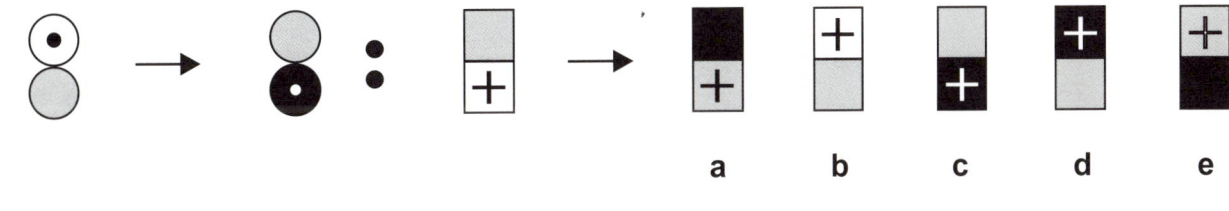
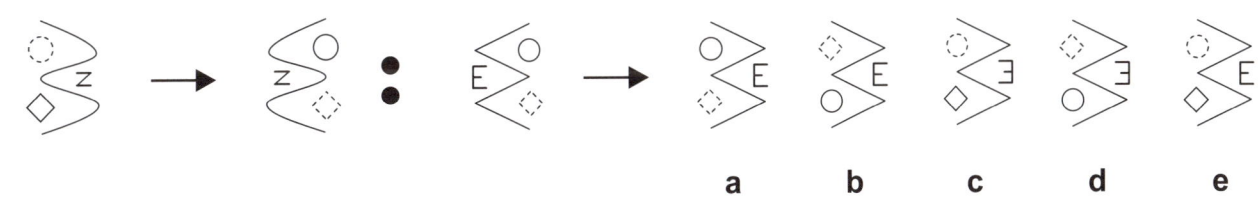
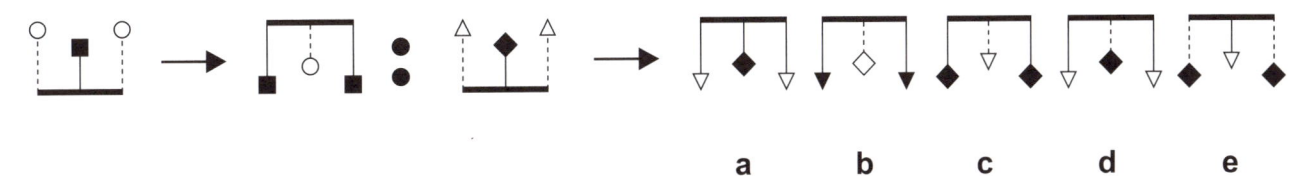

MOVE ON TO THE NEXT PAGE

9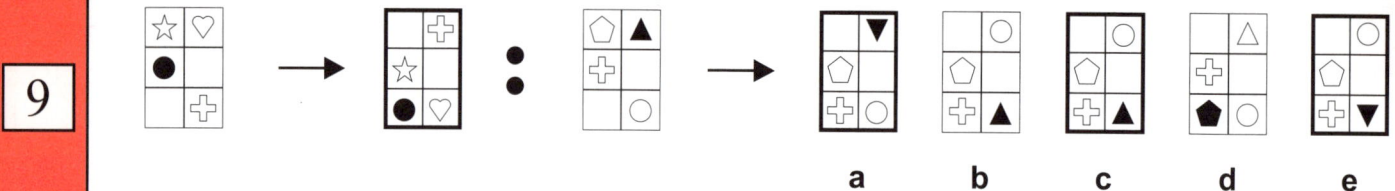

10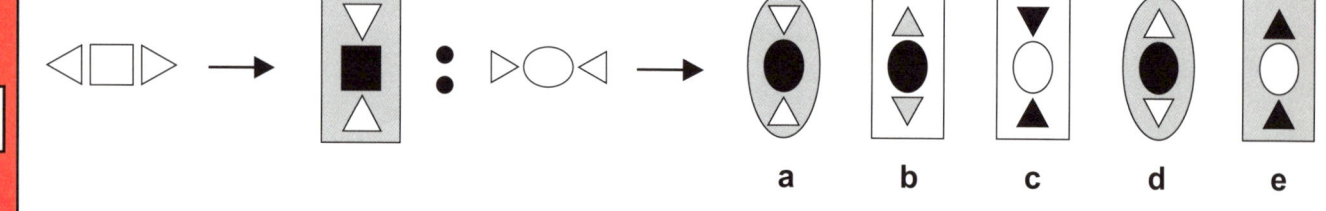

11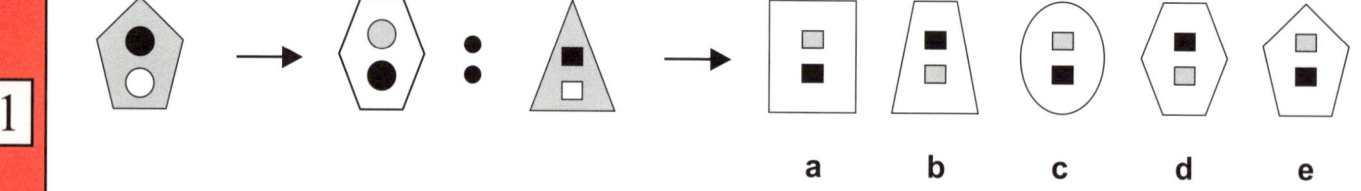

12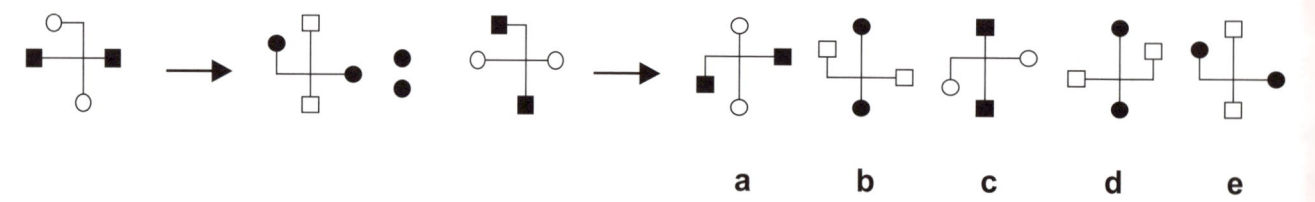

MOVE ON TO THE NEXT SECTION

Section D

In the questions below you will find five boxes on the left-hand side of the page. These boxes are arranged in order.

One of the boxes has been left empty.

You must choose one of the boxes from the right hand side that will take the place of the empty box and circle the correct letter below it, or mark the appropriate box on the multiple choice answer sheet.

Example:

a (b) c d e

Answer: b.

1

a b c d e

2

a b c d e

3

a b c d e

4

a b c d e

MOVE ON TO THE NEXT PAGE

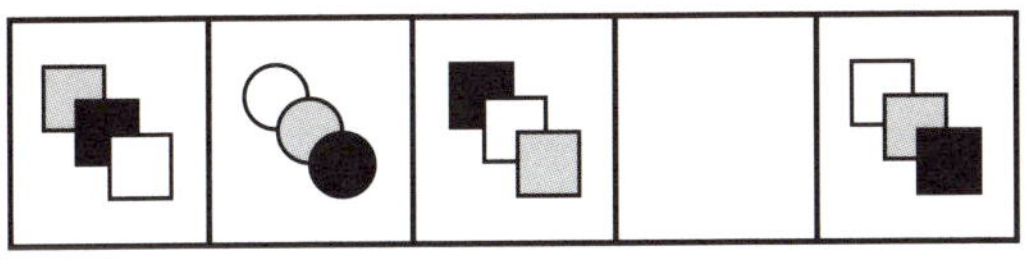

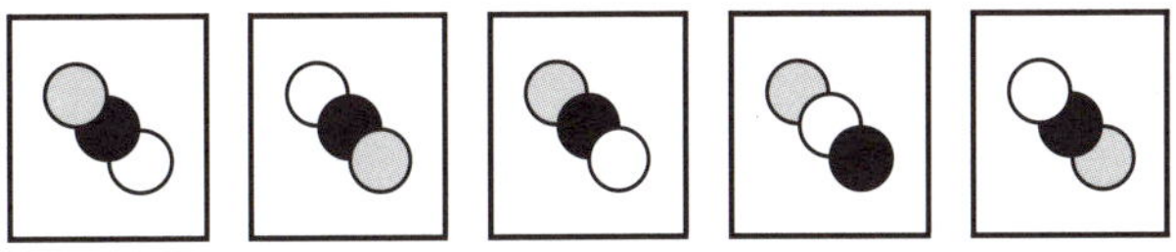

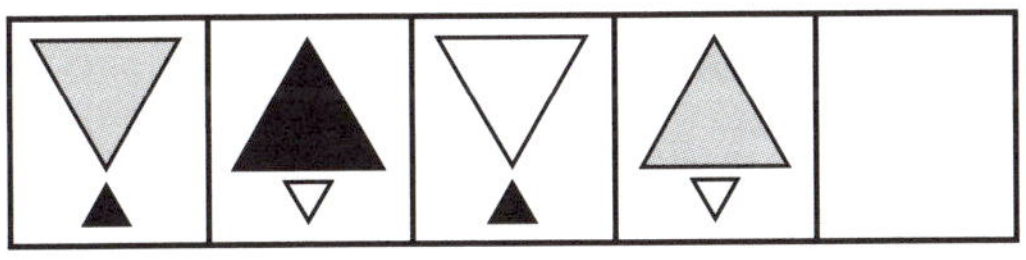

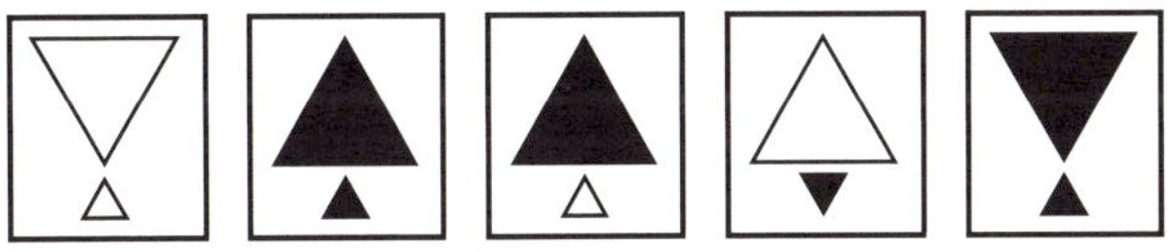

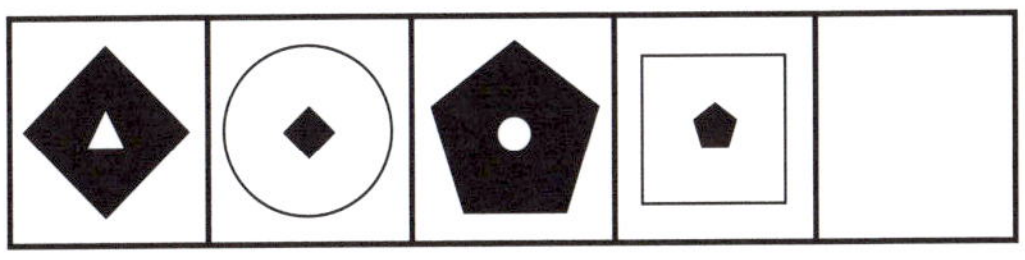

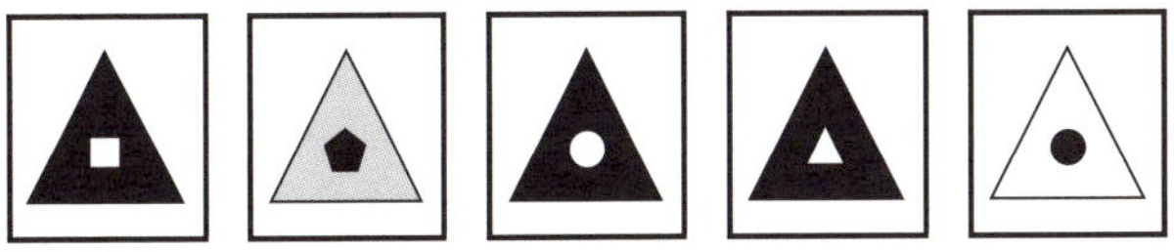

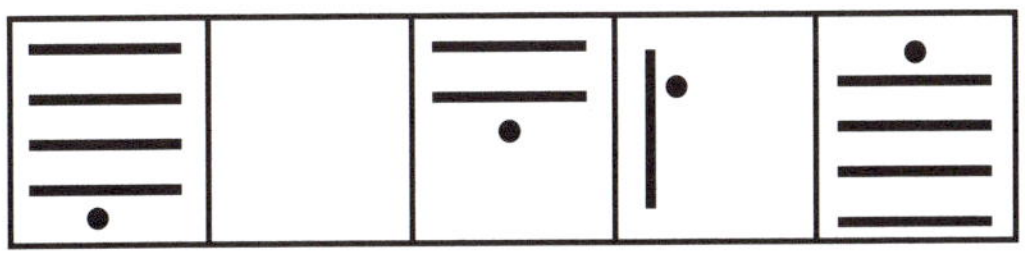

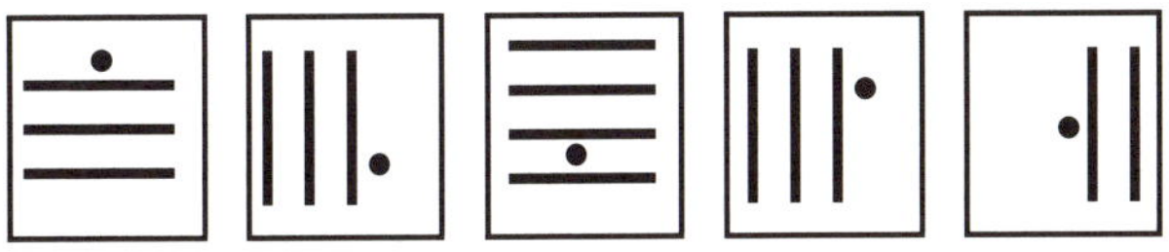

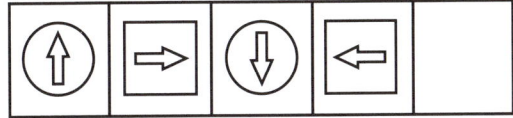

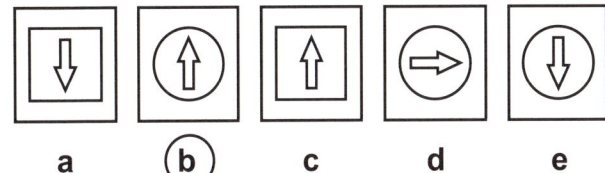

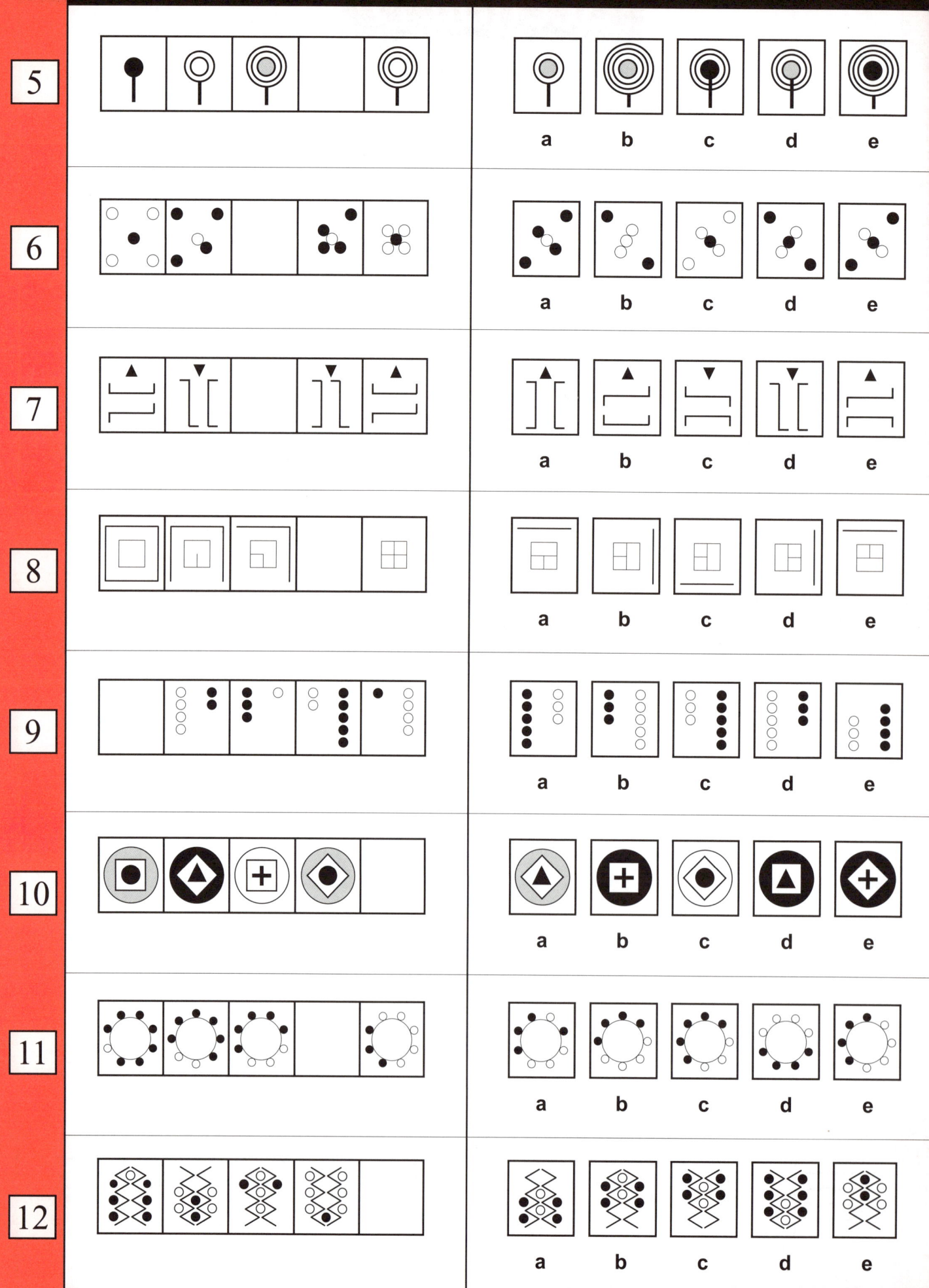

Section E

In the following questions there are two shapes on the left-hand side that are similar in some way.
On the right-hand side there are five other shapes.

You must decide which **one** of the five shapes is most like the pair on the left side of the page. Circle the letter under the shape, or mark the appropriate box on the multiple choice answer sheet.

Example

a b c d (e)

Answer: e

1

a b c d e

2

a b c d e

3

a b c d e

MOVE ON TO THE NEXT PAGE

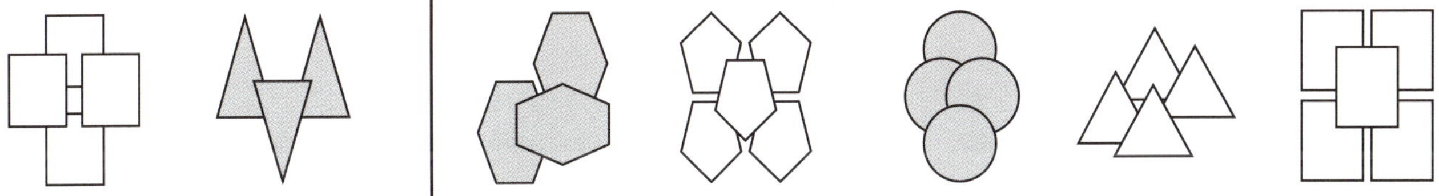

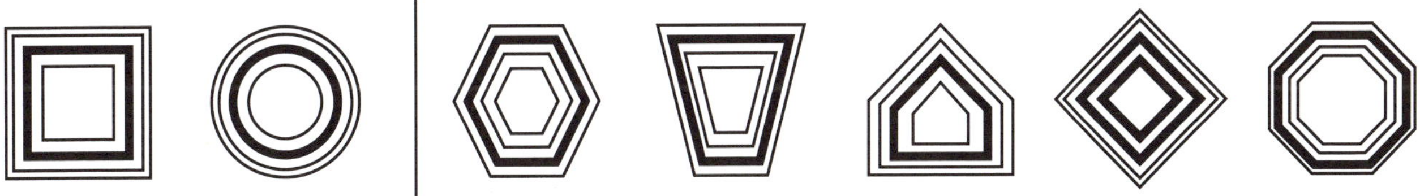

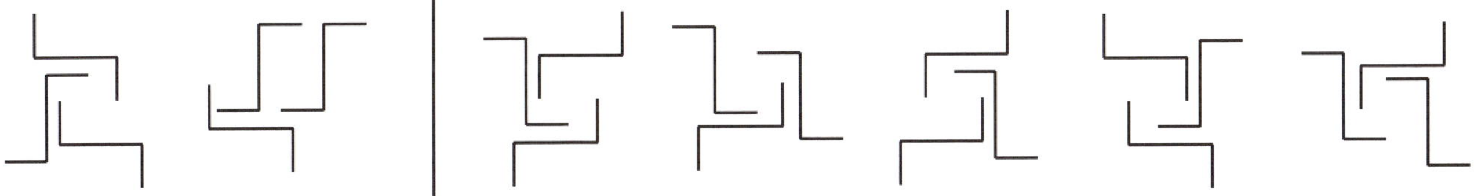

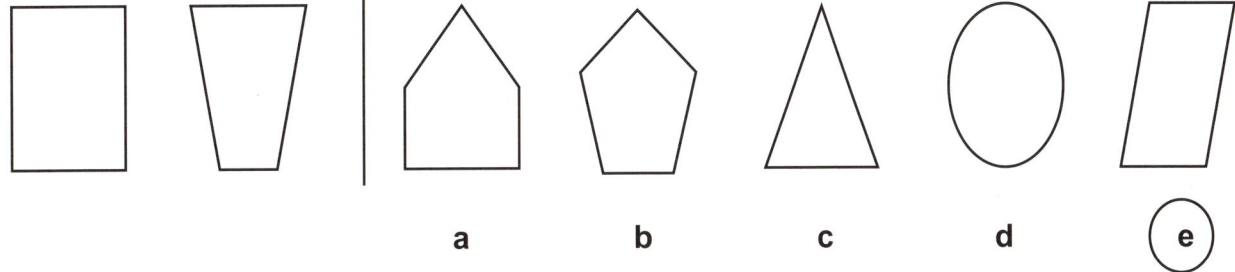

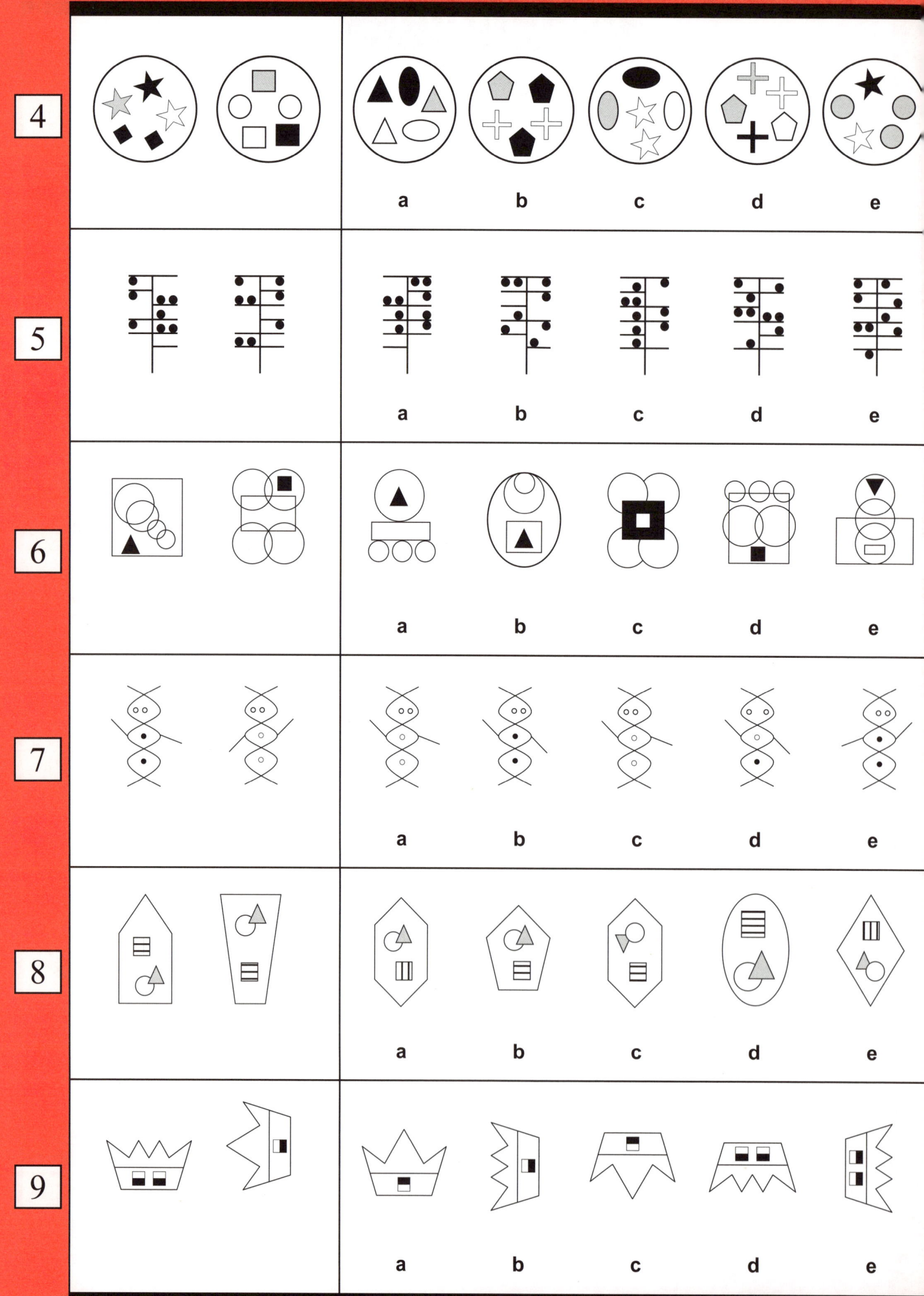

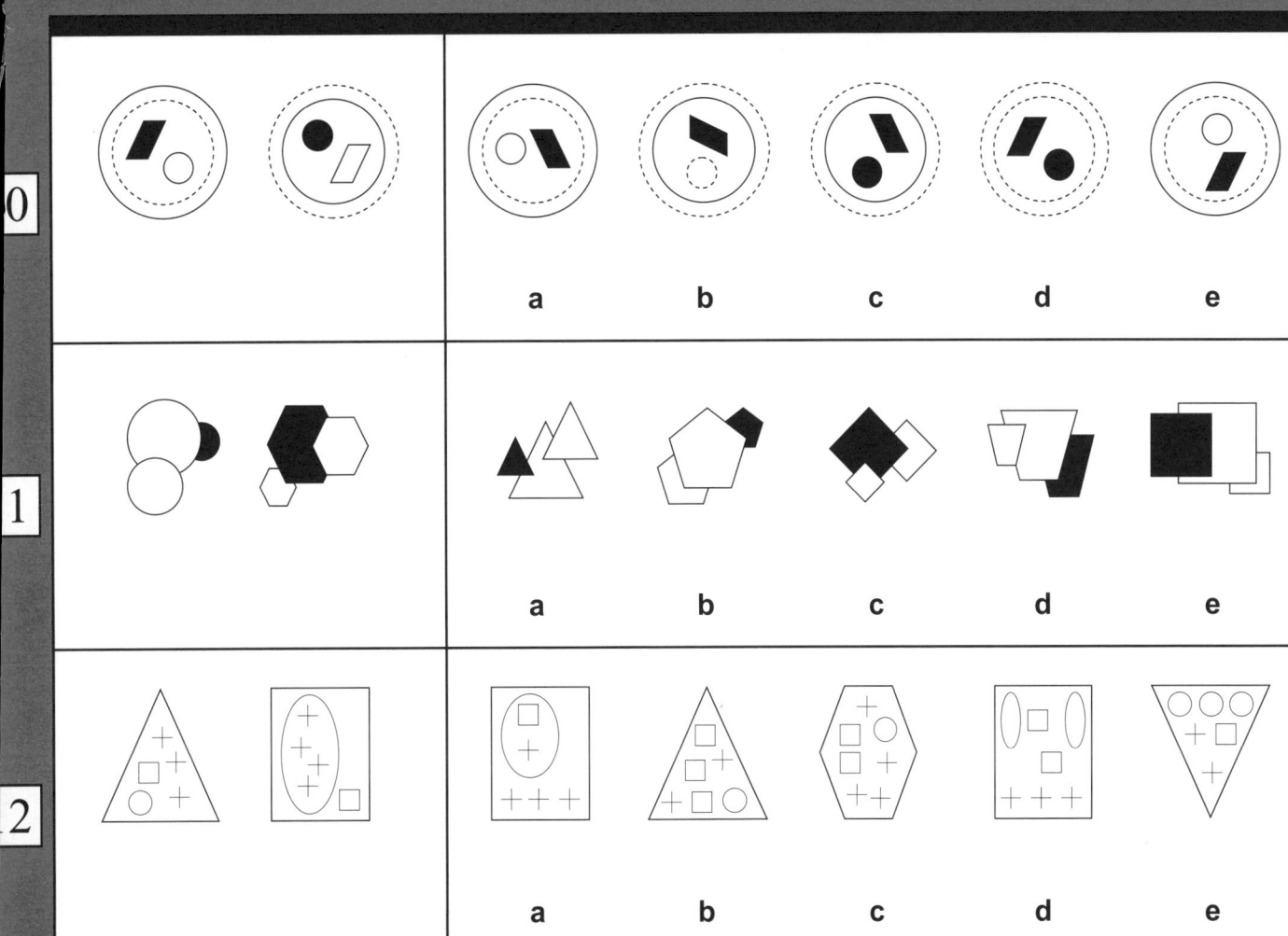

Eleven Plus Exam Group

Eleven Plus
Practice Paper

Non-Verbal Reasoning

Paper NVR 3

<u>Dual Format</u>
<u>Standard and Multiple choice</u>

60 Questions to be completed in 50 minutes

Name: _____

Date: _____

Score: _____

© Eleven Plus Exam Group 2010

Section A

In the questions below there are two shapes on the left-hand side of the page. These shapes are separated by an arrow. Look carefully and try to decide how the pair are related.

After this pair there is a third shape, followed by an arrow, and then five more shapes.
You must decide which of the group of five shapes goes with the **third shape** to make a pair, like the pair on the left of the page.

Circle the letter under the shape, or mark the appropriate box on the multiple choice answer sheet.

Example

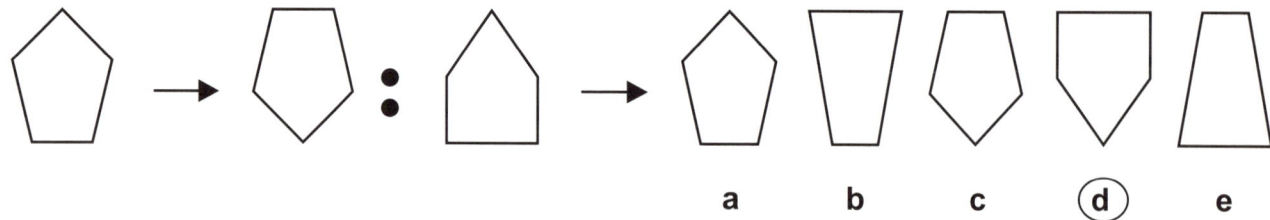

Answer: d

1.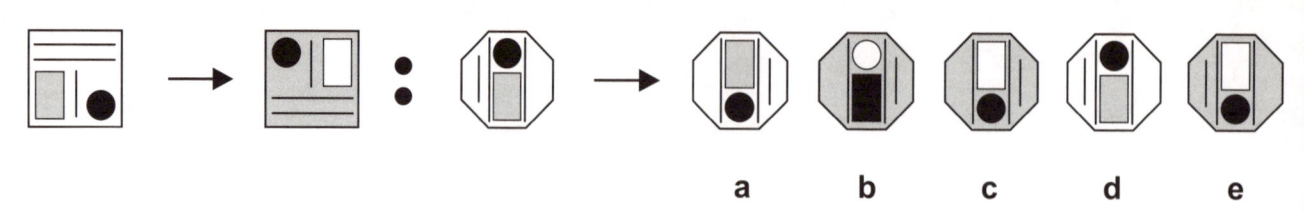

2.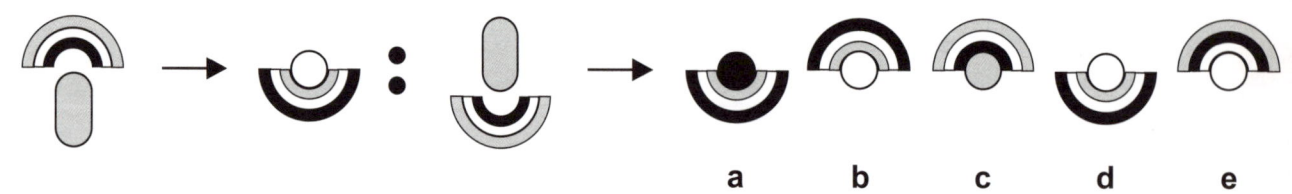

MOVE ON TO THE NEXT PAGE

3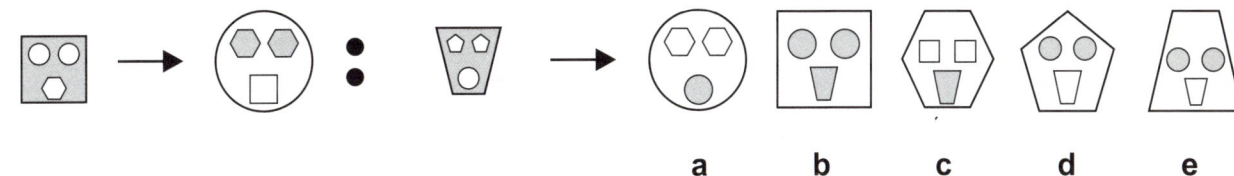

4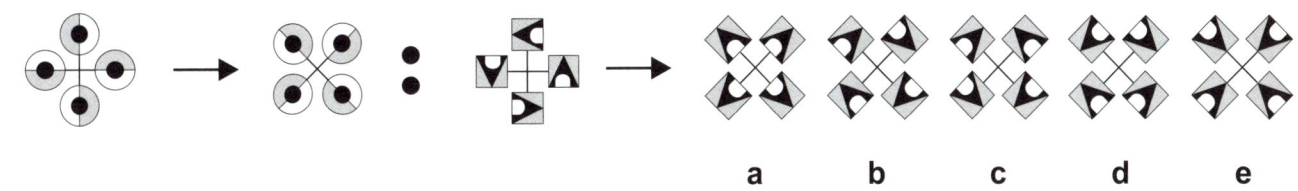

5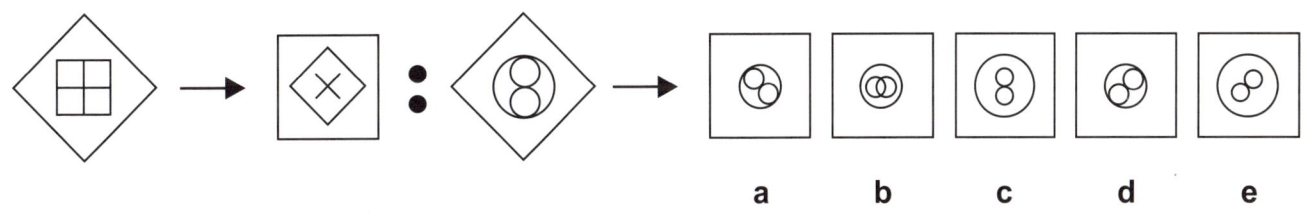

6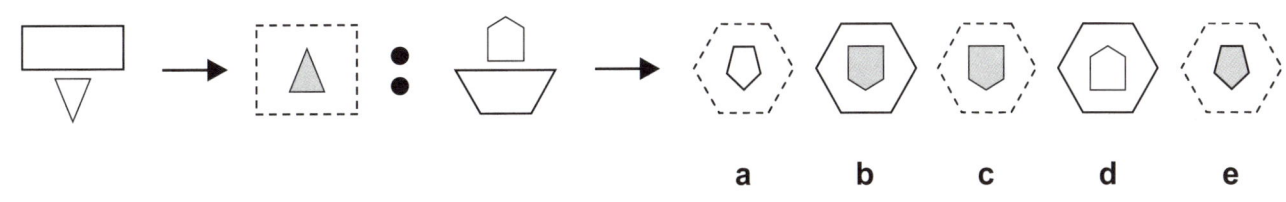

7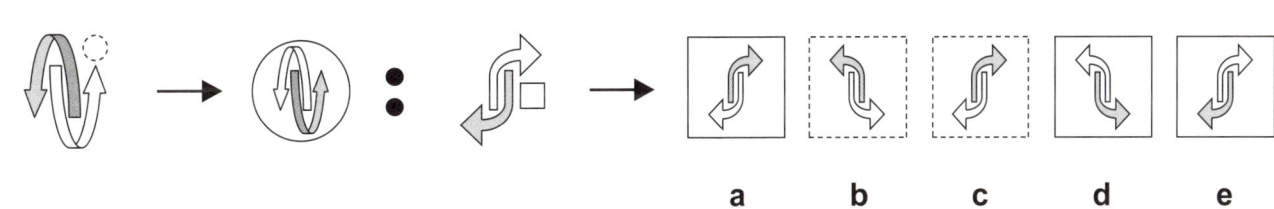

8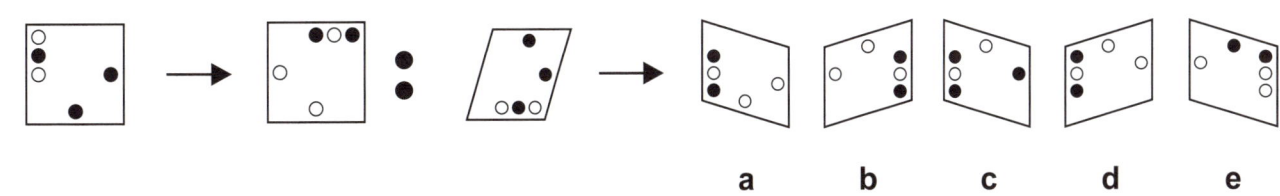

MOVE ON TO THE NEXT PAGE

9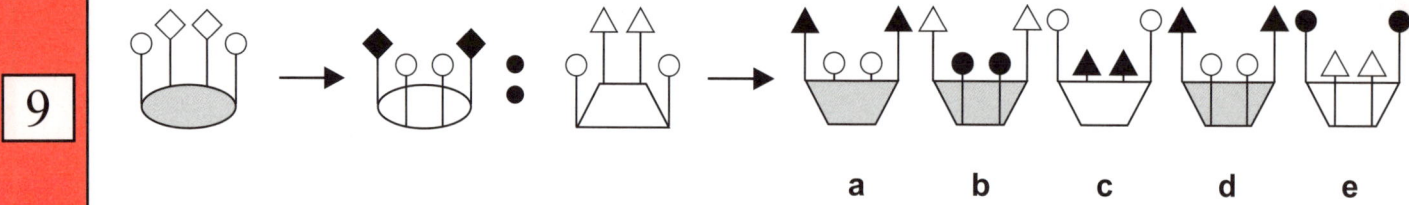

10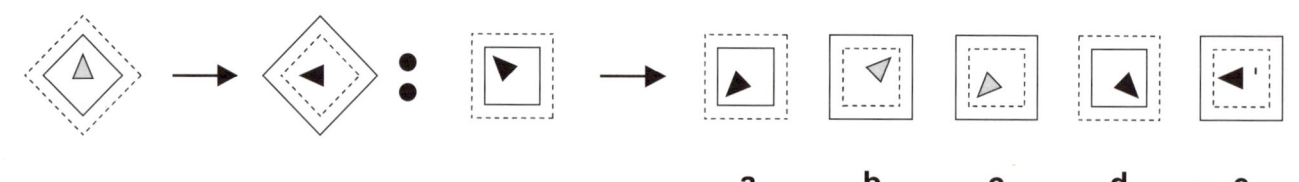

11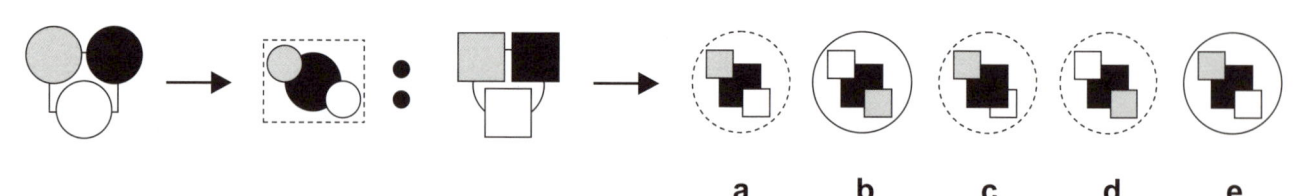

MOVE ON TO THE NEXT SECTION

Section B

In the questions below you will find five boxes on the left-hand side of the page. These boxes are arranged in order.

One of the boxes has been left empty.

You must choose one of the boxes from the right hand side that will take the place of the empty box and circle the correct letter below it, or mark the appropriate box on the multiple choice answer sheet.

Example:

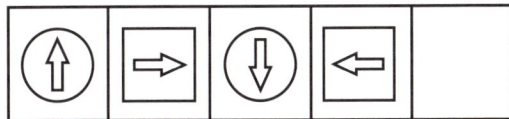

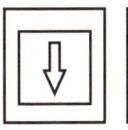 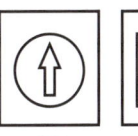 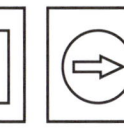 

a   b   c   d   e

Answer: b.

1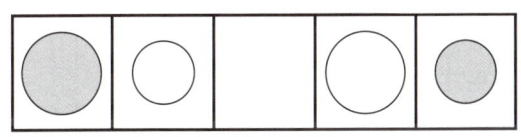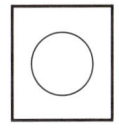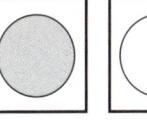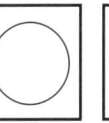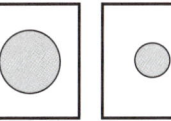

a   b   c   d   e

2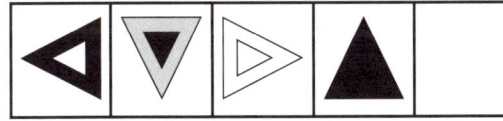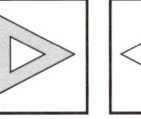

a   b   c   d   e

3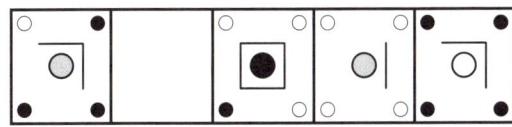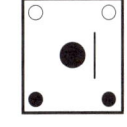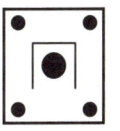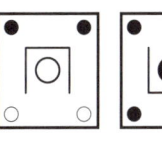

a   b   c   d   e

4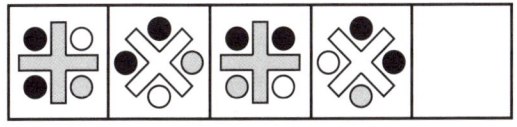

a   b   c   d   e

MOVE ON TO THE NEXT PAGE

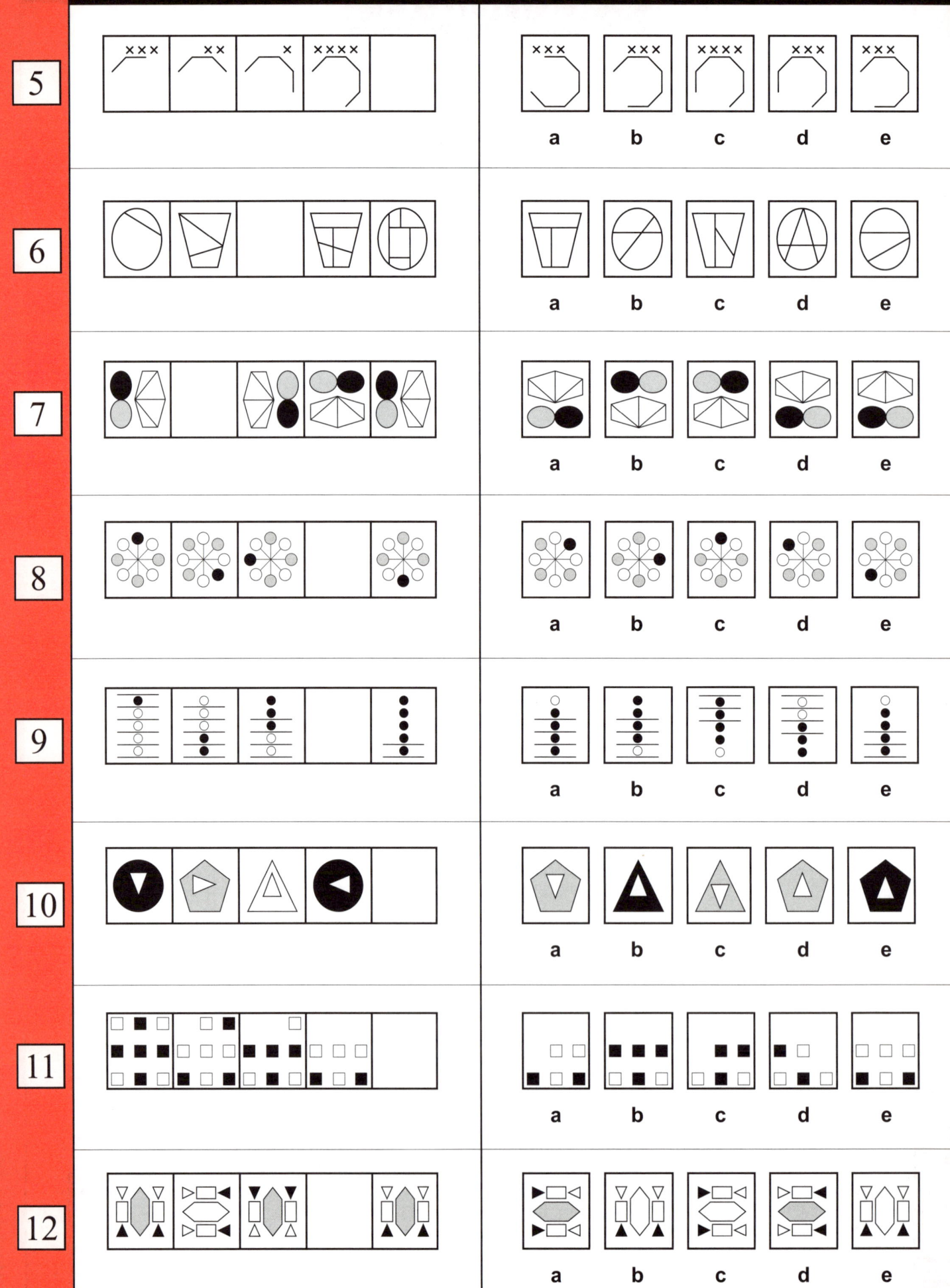

Section C

To answer the following questions you will need to work out a code. On the left-hand side of the page there are some shapes and their codes. You must work out how the letter codes go with the shapes.

Using this information you must choose one of the codes from the right hand side that best describes the shape without a code. Circle the correct letter below it, or mark the appropriate box on the multiple choice answer sheet.

Example 1

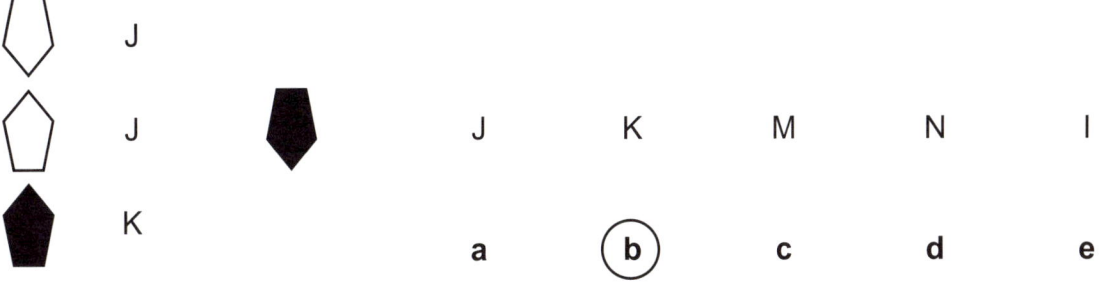

Answer: b

Two of the shapes have the code letter J. What makes these similar is that they are not shaded. The shaded shape has the code letter K. Therefore the un-coded shape must have the code letter K as it is shaded and the answer is **b**.

Example 2

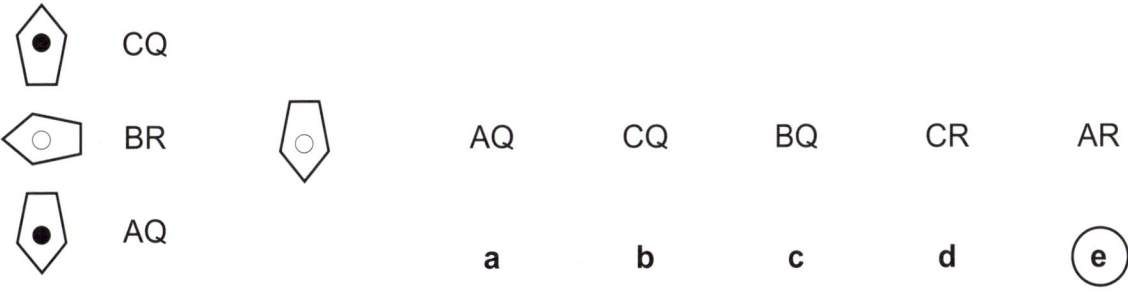

Answer: e

In this example each shape has two code letters. The first letter of each code refers to one aspect of the shape. Each shape has a different letter **A**, **B**, and **C**. What is different about each of the shapes? They are each turned in a different direction. The uncoded shape points in the same direction as **A**, so its code letter must be **A**.

The second code letter refers to another aspect of the shape. Two of the shapes have the code **Q**. What is the same in the shapes? They both have black circles, whereas the shape with the code **R** has a white circle. The uncoded shape has a white circle, and therefore the second code letter must be **R**.

Now we can tell that the code for the uncoded shape must be **AR**.

1

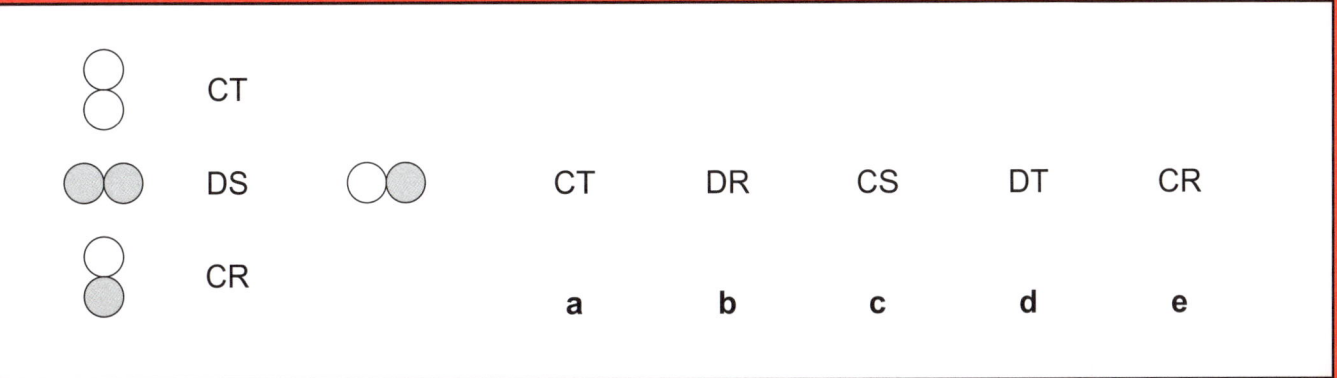

MOVE ON TO THE NEXT PAGE

© Eleven Plus exam Group 2010

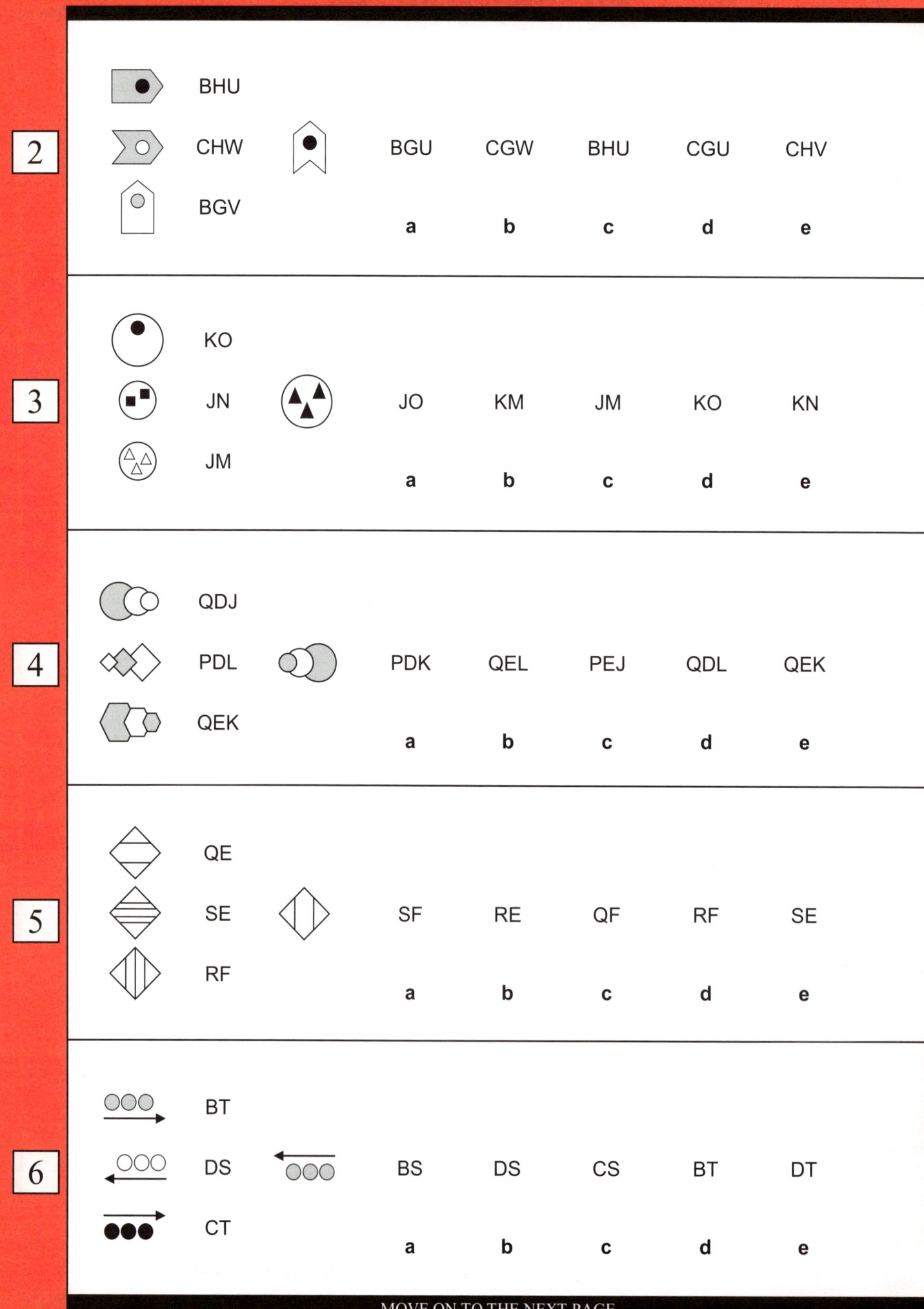

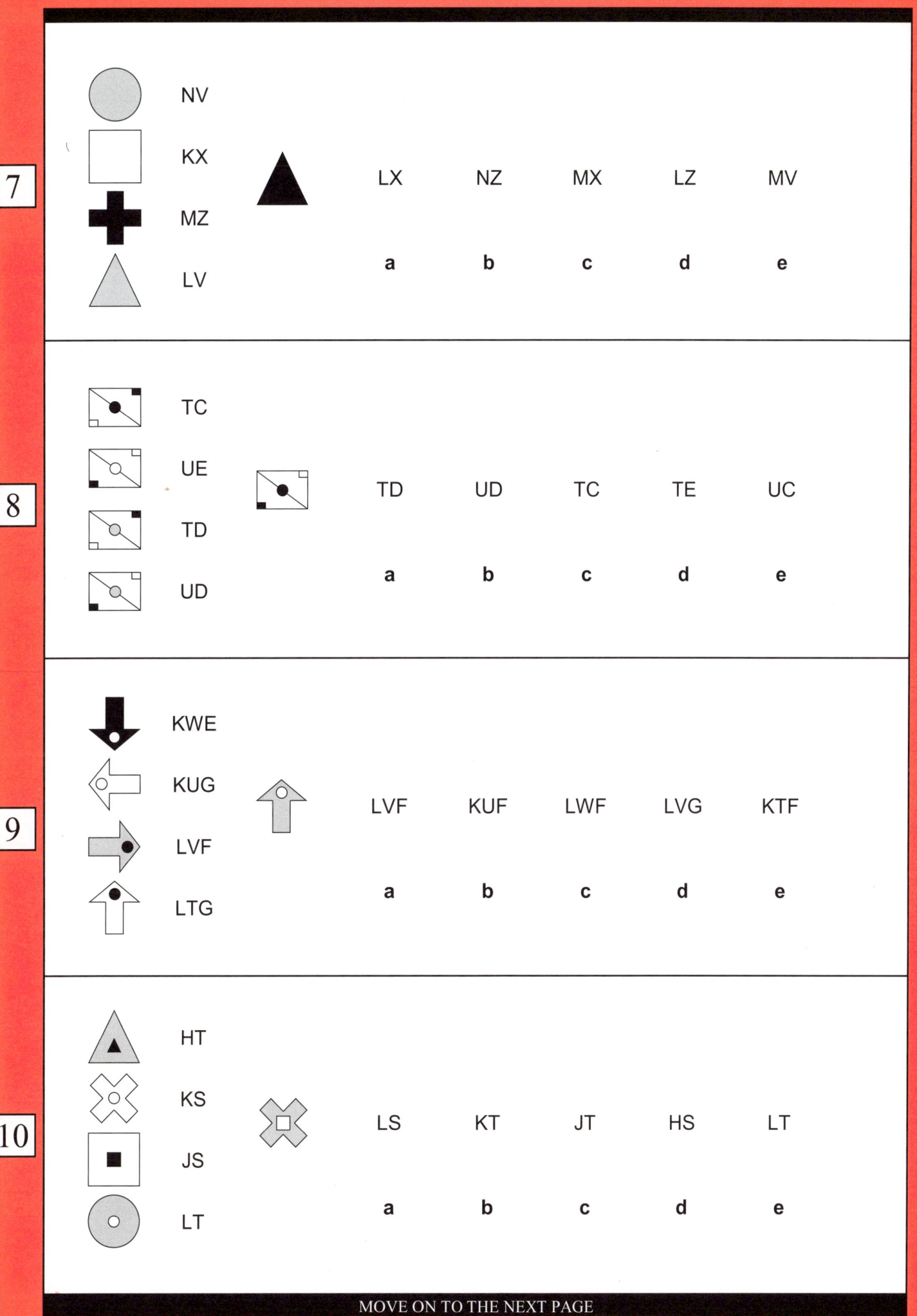

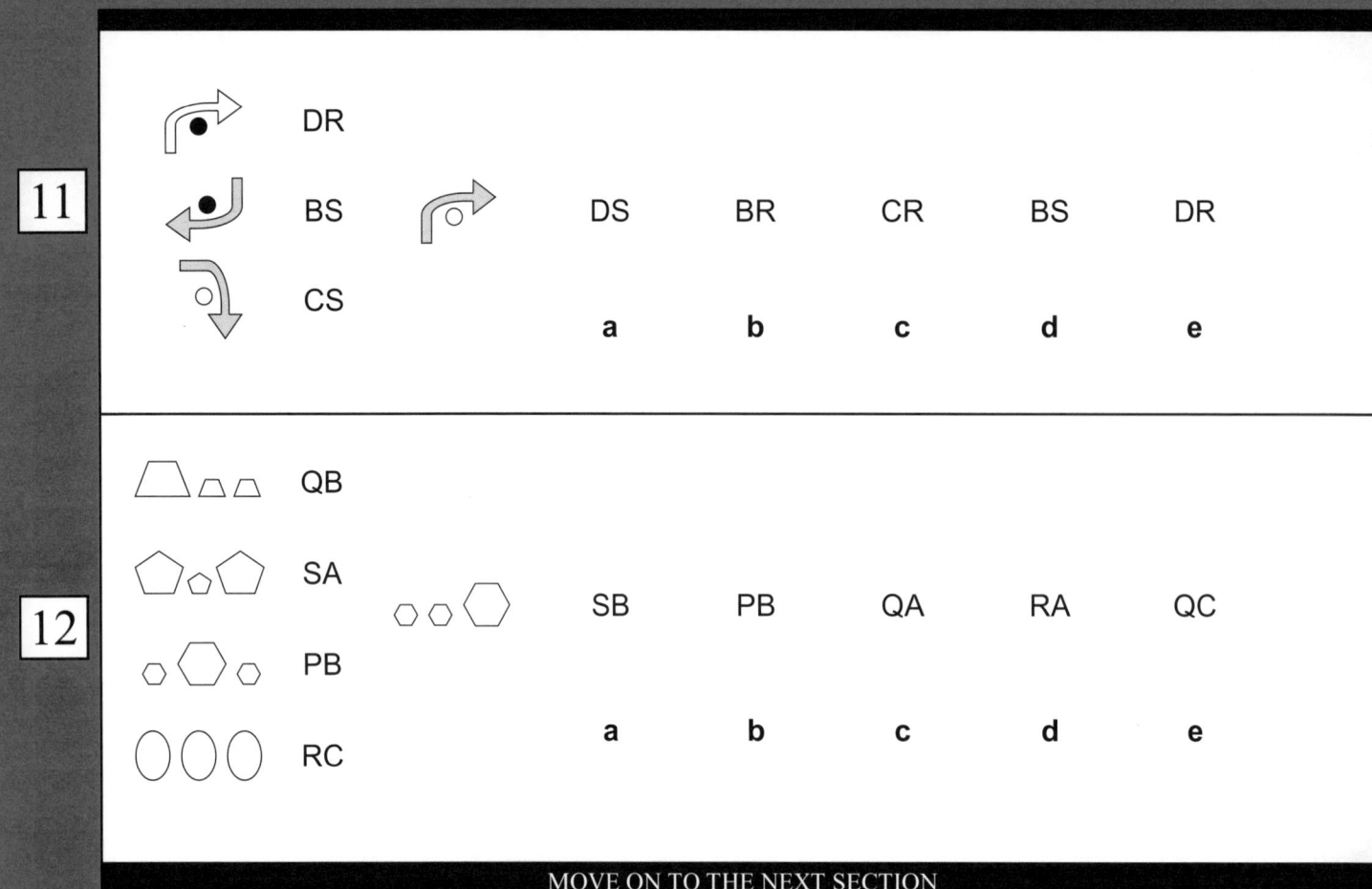

Section D

In the following questions there is a large square made up of smaller ones.
One of the smaller squares has been left blank.

You must choose one of the boxes from the right hand side that will take the place of the empty box and complete the pattern. Circle the letter below it, or mark the appropriate box on the multiple choice answer sheet.

Example

 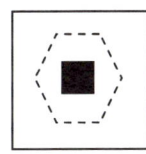 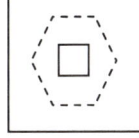   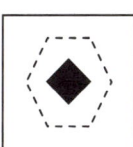

                                                    a   b   c   e

Answer: d

1

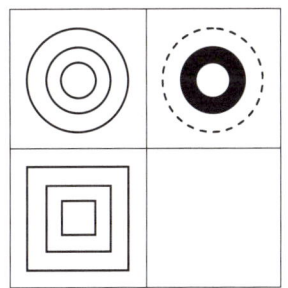 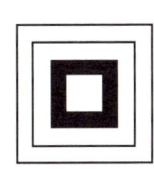   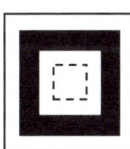 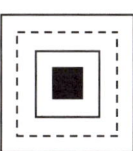

                                                    a   b   c   d   e

2

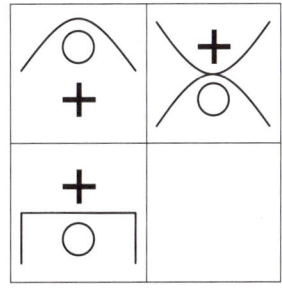 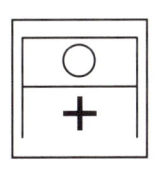 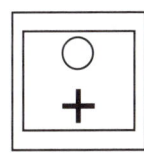 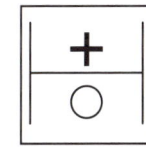 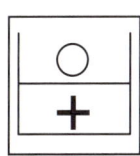 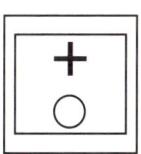

                                                  a   b   c   d   e

MOVE ON TO THE NEXT PAGE

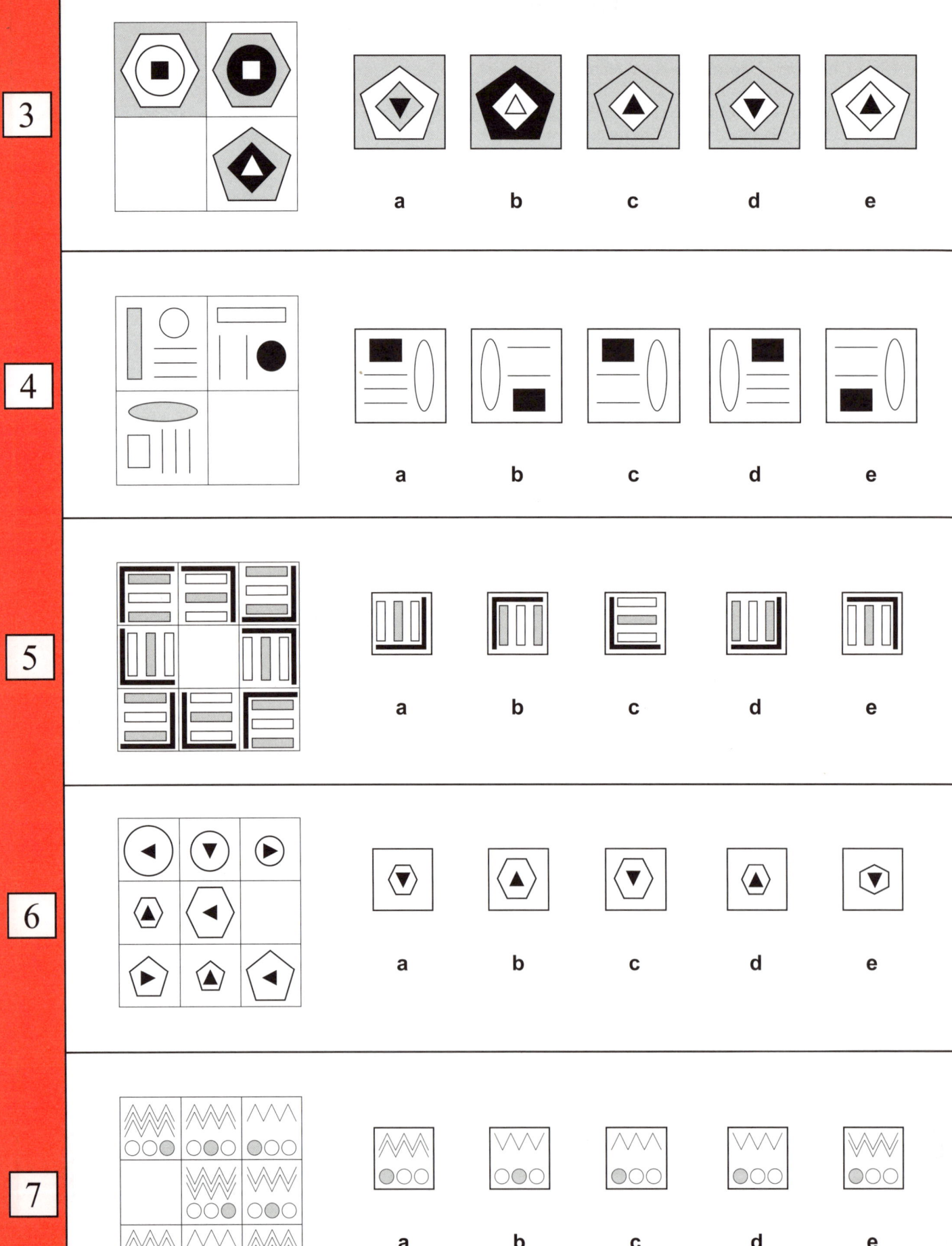

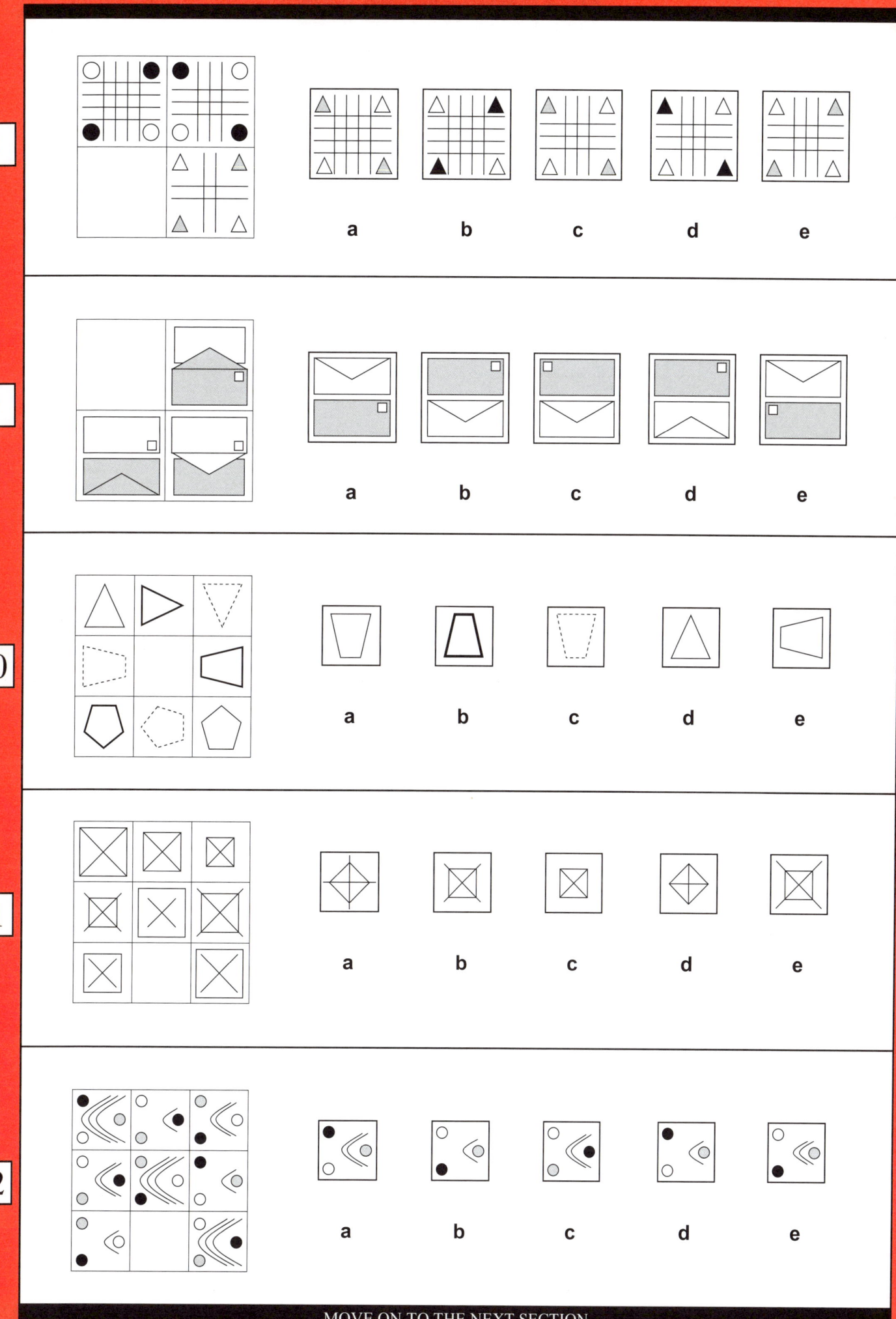

Section E

In each of the following questions you will find five figures.

You must find the one figure from the five that is **most unlike** the rest.

Circle the correct letter below, or mark the appropriate box on the multiple choice answer sheet.

Example:

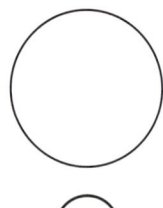 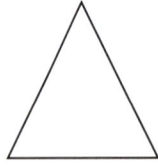 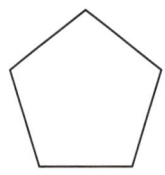  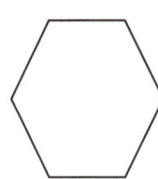

a   b   c   d   e

Answer: a

1 

a   b   c   d   e

2 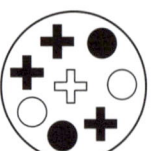

a   b   c   d   e

3 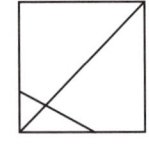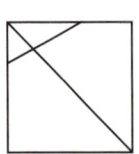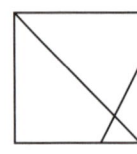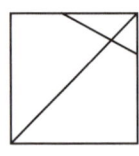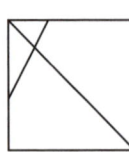

a   b   c   d   e

MOVE ON TO THE NEXT PAGE

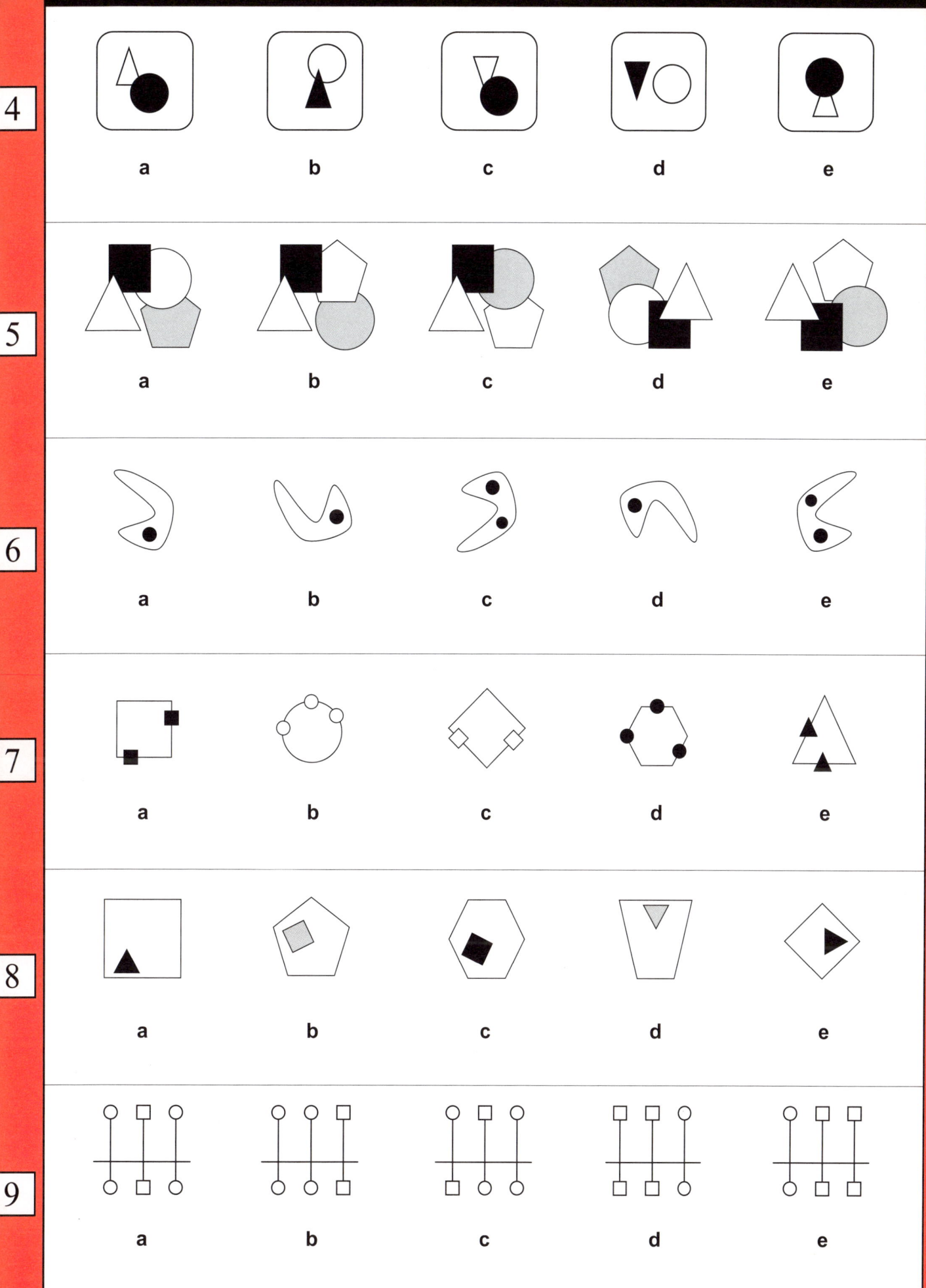

10

| a | b | c | d | e |

11

| a | b | c | d | e |

12

| a | b | c | d | e |

YOU ARE AT THE END OF THE TEST

Eleven Plus Exam Group

Eleven Plus Non-Verbal Reasoning Tests

Answers

NVR 1

Section A	Section B	Section C	Section D	Section E
1. D	1. C	1. D	1. D	1. B
2. A	2. B	2. A	2. C	2. C
3. D	3. D	3. D	3. A	3. E
4. B	4. A	4. A	4. E	4. E
5. C	5. D	5. C	5. B	5. A
6. E	6. C	6. B	6. D	6. B
7. C	7. B	7. A	7. C	7. C
8. B	8. A	8. E	8. B	8. D
9. E	9. B	9. D	9. E	9. B
10. E	10. E	10. C	10. E	10. A
11. C	11. B	11. D	11. D	11. B
12. A	12. C	12. D	12. B	12. B

NVR 2

Section A	Section B	Section C	Section D	Section E
1. C	1. B	1. B	1. E	1. C
2. D	2. E	2. E	2. C	2. E
3. A	3. A	3. D	3. B	3. A
4. D	4. A	4. D	4. A	4. E
5. C	5. D	5. A	5. D	5. C
6. E	6. C	6. E	6. E	6. B
7. A	7. C	7. B	7. A	7. E
8. E	8. E	8. B	8. B	8. B
9. B	9. E	9. D	9. B	9. A
10. C	10. D	10. C	10. C	10. D
11. E	11. E	11. C	11. E	11. D
12. B	12. A	12. E	12. D	12. C

Eleven Plus Exam Group

Eleven Plus Non-Verbal Reasoning Tests

Answers

NVR 3

Section A	Section B	Section C	Section D	Section E
1. C	1. E	1. B	1. C	1. C
2. B	2. C	2. D	2. B	2. D
3. D	3. D	3. B	3. E	3. B
4. B	4. B	4. C	4. C	4. D
5. E	5. B	5. C	5. B	5. B
6. C	6. B	6. A	6. C	6. A
7. C	7. D	7. D	7. D	7. D
8. A	8. A	8. E	8. C	8. C
9. D	9. E	9. E	9. A	9. C
10. E	10. A	10. B	10. A	10. E
11. C	11. C	11. A	11. E	11. D
12. A	12. C	12. B	12. A	12. A

NVR 4

Section A	Section B	Section C	Section D	Section E
1. C	1. A	1. B	1. C	1. B
2. D	2. E	2. A	2. E	2. C
3. B	3. C	3. D	3. A	3. D
4. D	4. B	4. C	4. B	4. C
5. C	5. D	5. B	5. E	5. B
6. D	6. D	6. D	6. C	6. A
7. D	7. C	7. E	7. E	7. C
8. B	8. B	8. C	8. B	8. B
9. E	9. A	9. C	9. A	9. C
10. A	10. E	10. D	10. D	10. E
11. C	11. B	11. A	11. E	11. E
12. B	12. E	12. B	12. B	12. A

Eleven Plus Exam Group

Eleven Plus
Practice Paper

Non-Verbal Reasoning

Paper NVR 2

Dual Format
Standard and Multiple choice

60 Questions to be completed in 50 minutes

Name: _____

Date: _____

Score: _____

© Eleven Plus Exam Group 2010

Section A

To answer the following questions you will need to work out a code. In the boxes to the left of the page are shapes and code letters. The top letter in each box refers to one aspect of the shape, the bottom letter goes with another. You need to decide how the letters and shapes go together.

Now look at the shape on the right hand side of the page. You must choose one of the pairs of code letters to fill the empty spaces and circle the letter below it, or mark the appropriate box on the multiple choice answer sheet.

Example 1:

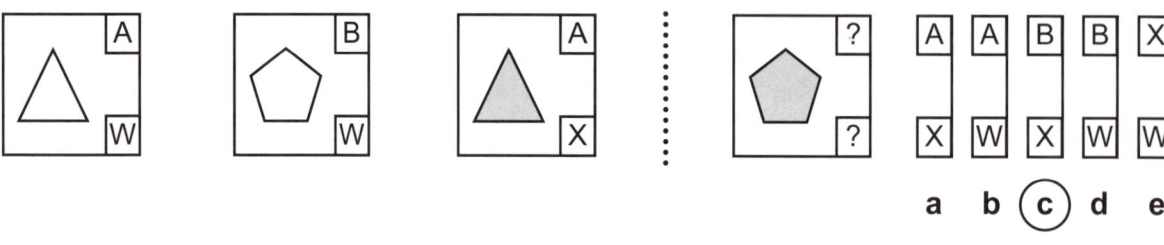

Answer: c

On the top row the code letter **A** appears twice. What is similar about these two shapes? They are both triangles. The code letter **W** appears twice below the shapes. What is similar about these shapes? They are both unshaded. Looking at the mystery shape we can see that it is a pentagon, which means that the first code letter should be **B**. It is also shaded, which means that the second code letter should be **X**. Therefore the answer is c. **BX**

Example 2:

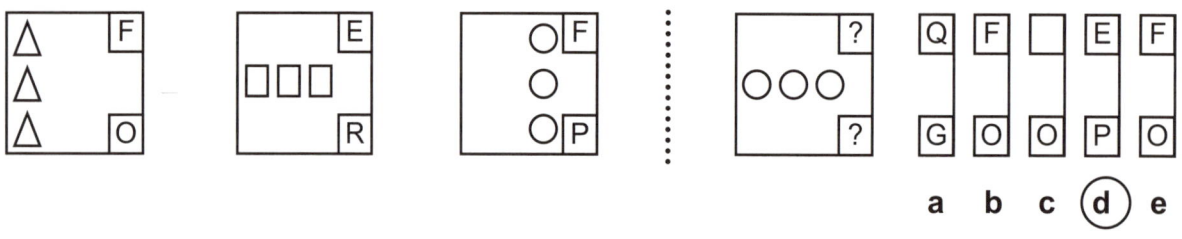

Answer: d

On the top row the code letter **F** appears twice. What is similar about these two shapes? They are both vertical. The code letter **P** appears only once below the shapes. All three code letters are different. What is different about all three shapes? They are formed from different shapes. Looking at the mystery box we can see the shape is horizontal, which means that the first code letter must be **E**. Its shape is a circle, and so the second code letter must be **P**. Therefore the answer is c. **EP**

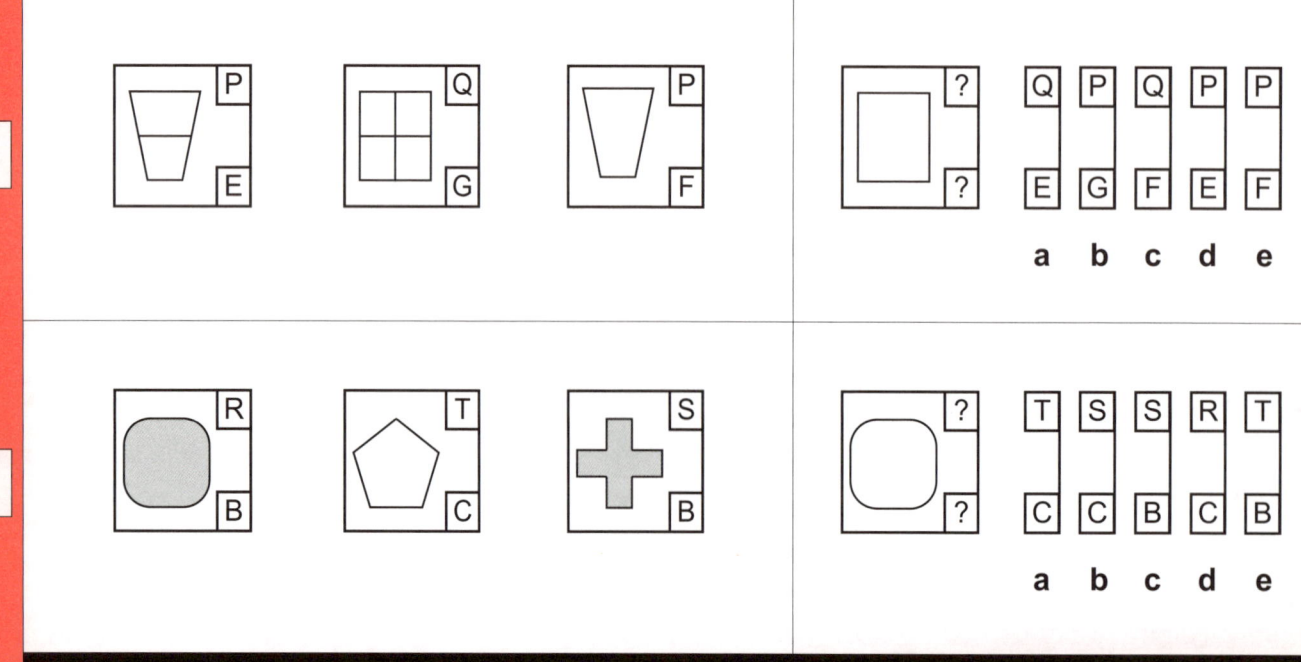

MOVE ON TO THE NEXT PAGE

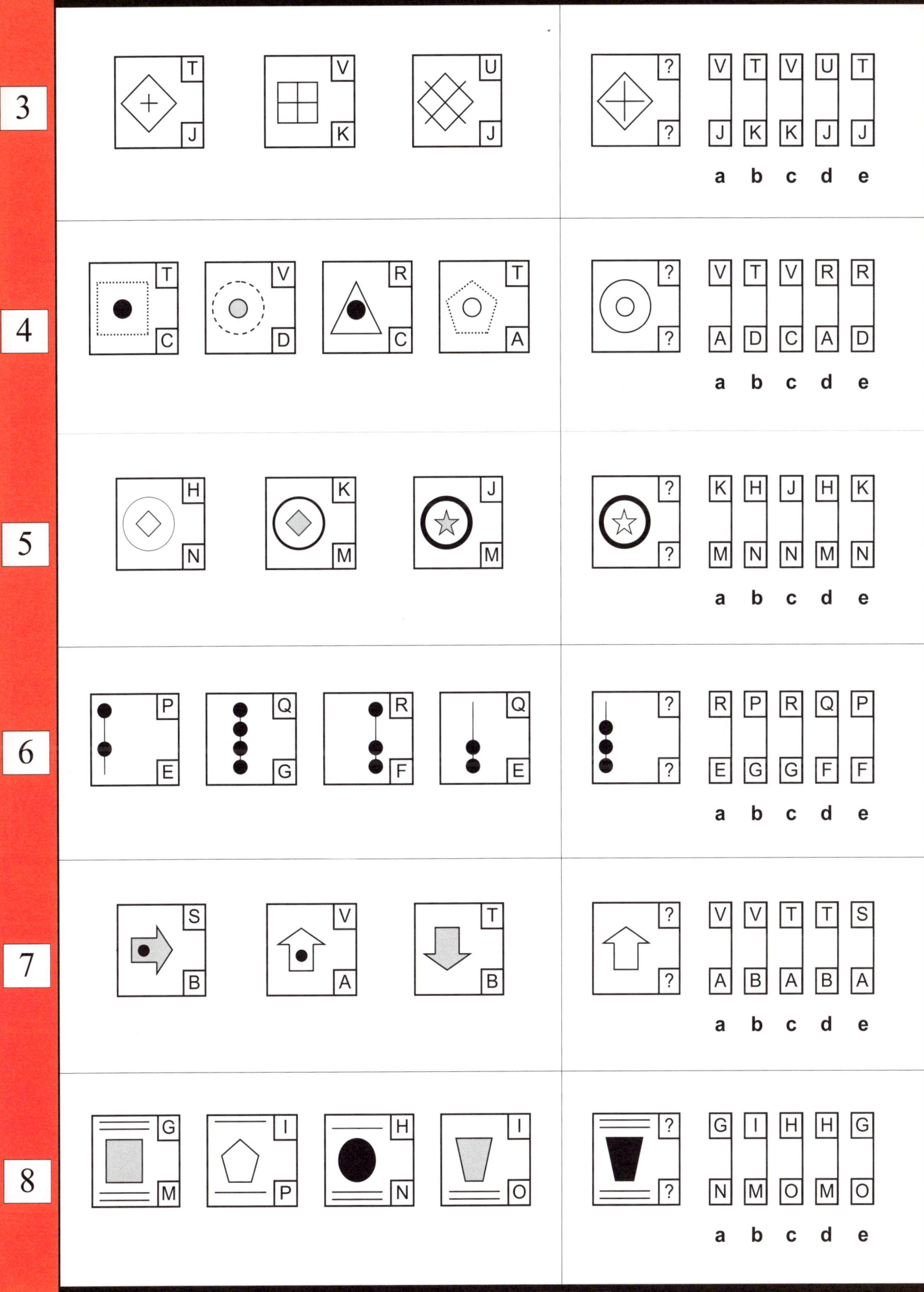

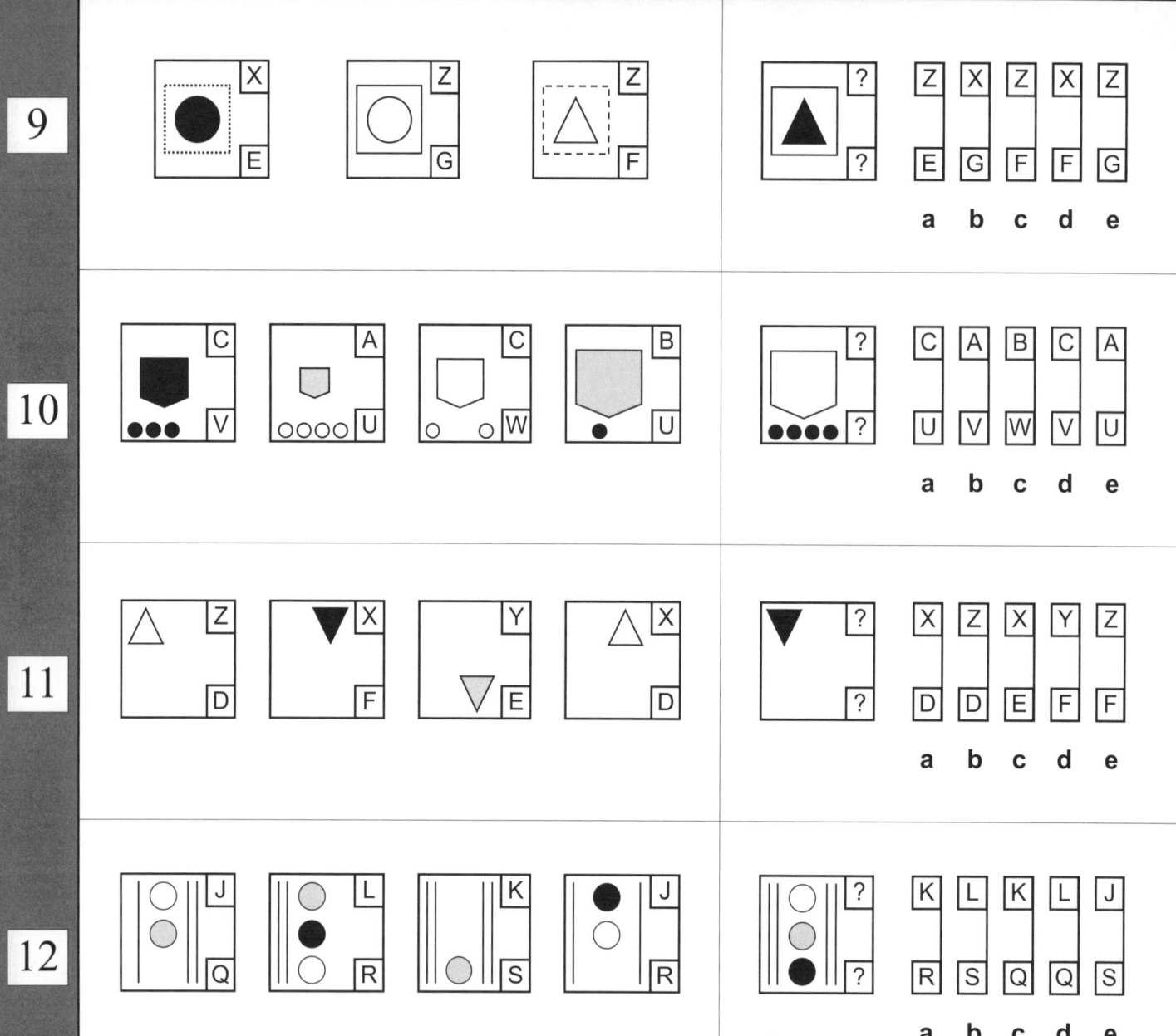

Section B

In each of the following questions you will find five figures.

You must find the one figure from the five that is **most unlike** the rest.

Circle the correct letter below, or mark the appropriate box on the multiple choice answer sheet.

Example:

  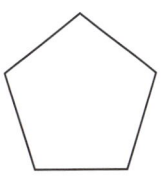 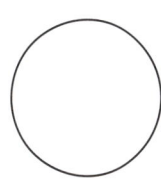 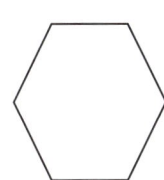

a　　　　　b　　　　　c　　　　　d　　　　　e

Answer: d

1　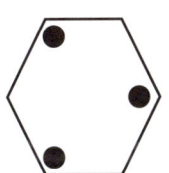

　　a　　　　　b　　　　　c　　　　　d　　　　　e

2　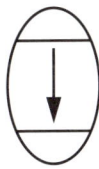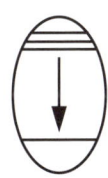

　　a　　　　　b　　　　　c　　　　　d　　　　　e

3　

　　a　　　　　b　　　　　c　　　　　d　　　　　e

MOVE ON TO THE NEXT PAGE

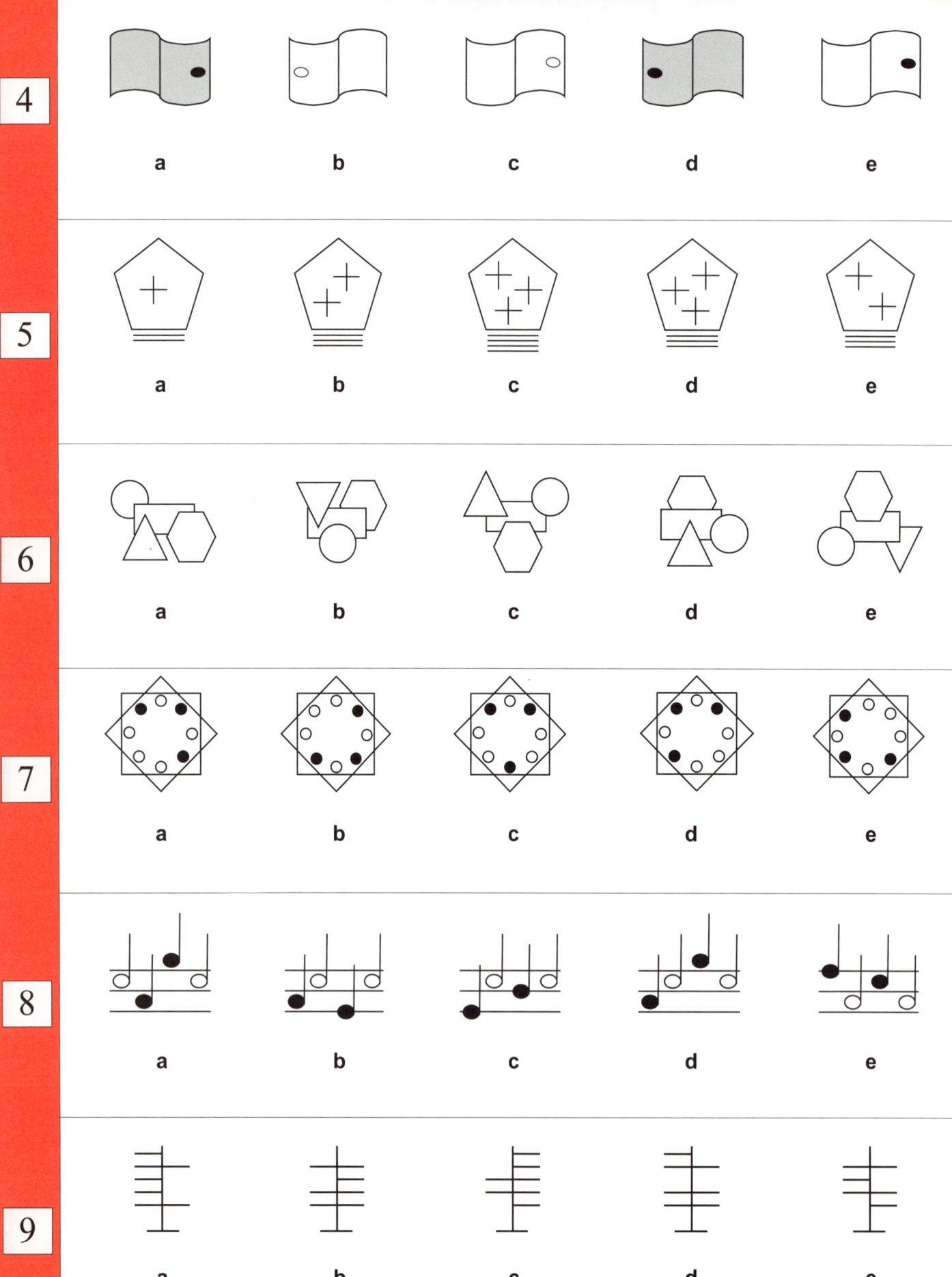

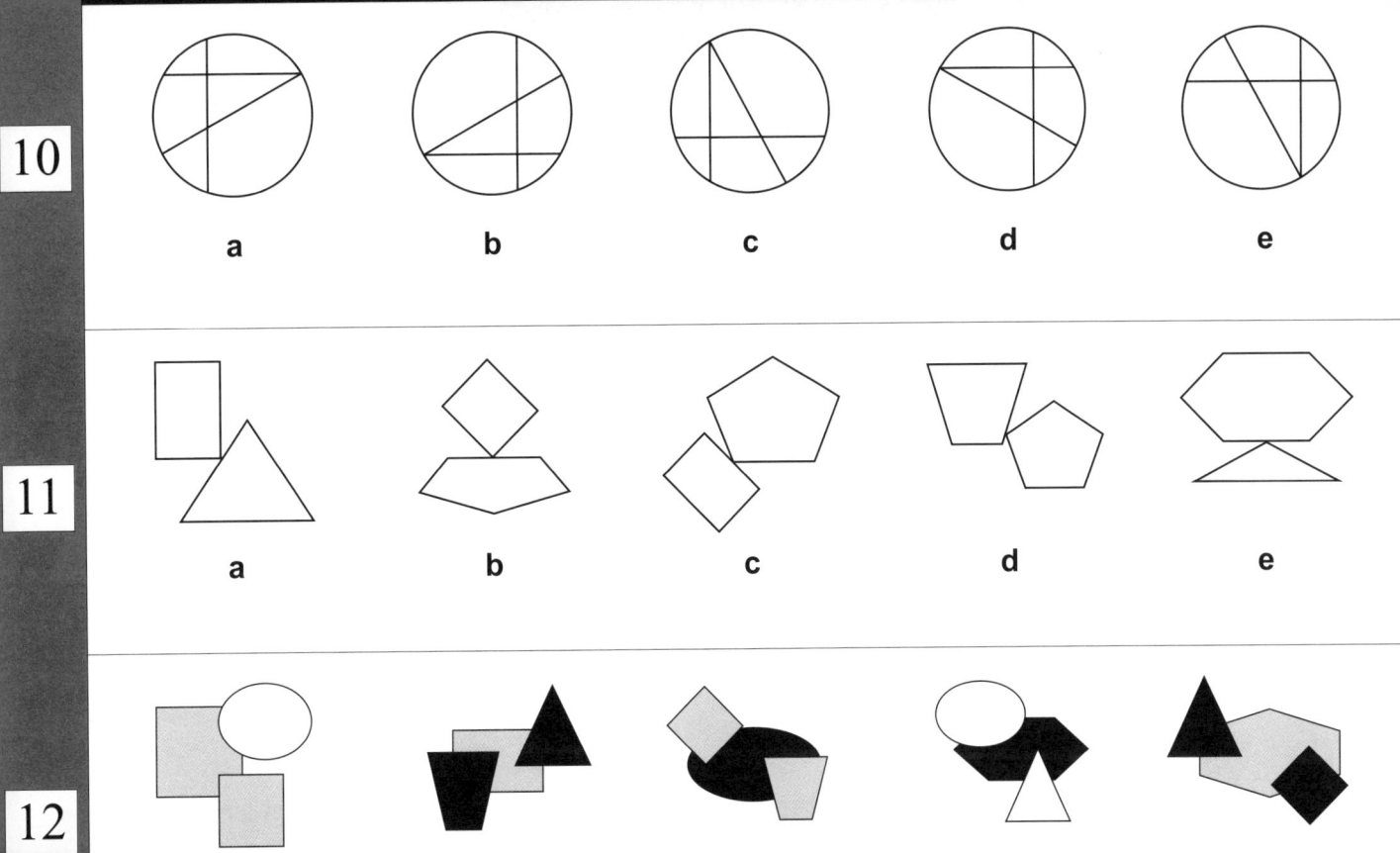

Section C

In the questions below there are two shapes on the left-hand side of the page. These shapes are separated by an arrow. Look carefully and try to decide how the pair are related.

After this pair there is a third shape, followed by an arrow, and then five more shapes.
You must decide which of the group of five shapes goes with the **third shape** to make a pair, like the pair on the left of the page.

Circle the letter under the shape, or mark the appropriate box on the multiple choice answer sheet.

Example

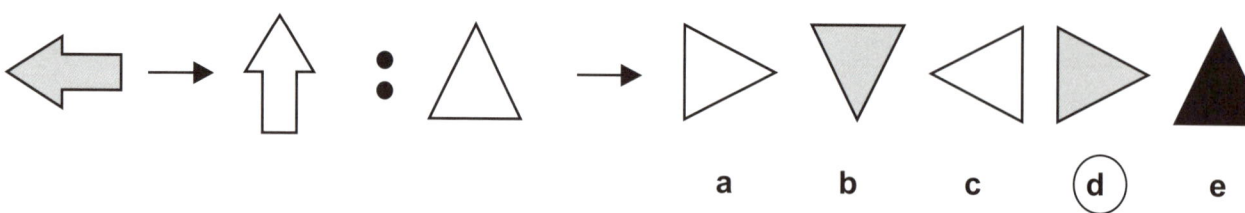

Answer: d

1
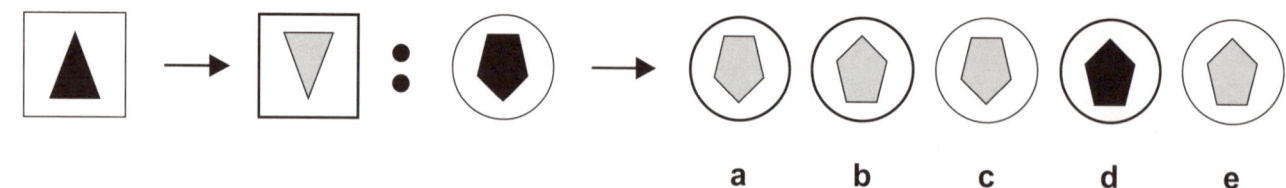

2
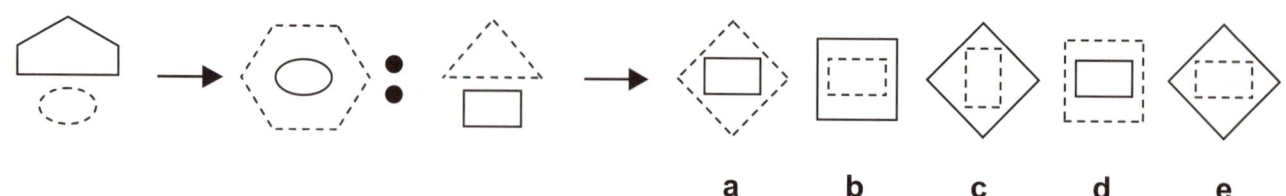

MOVE ON TO THE NEXT PAGE

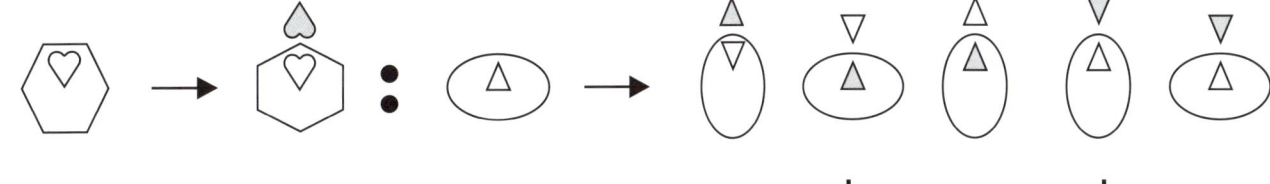
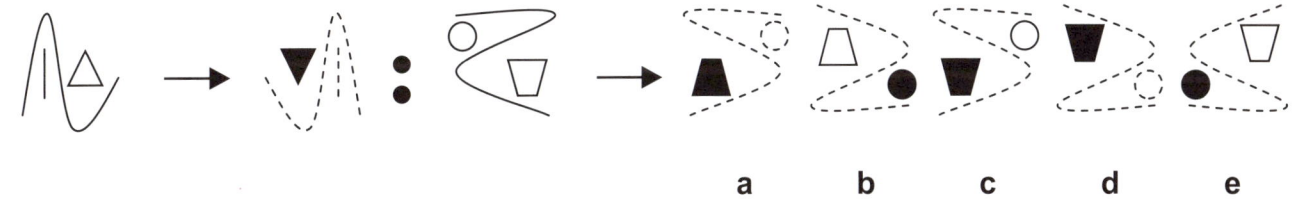
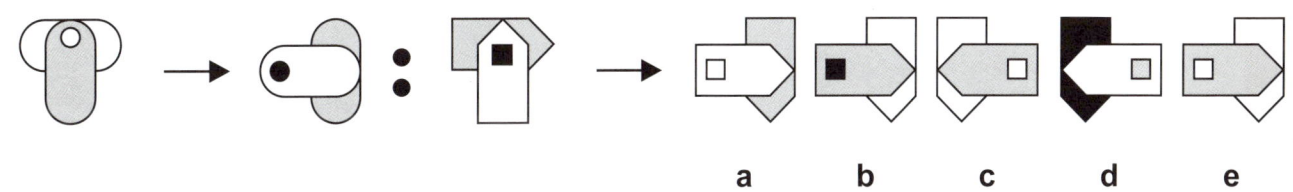
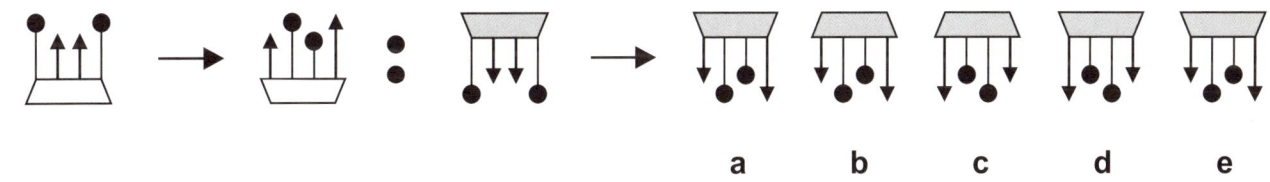
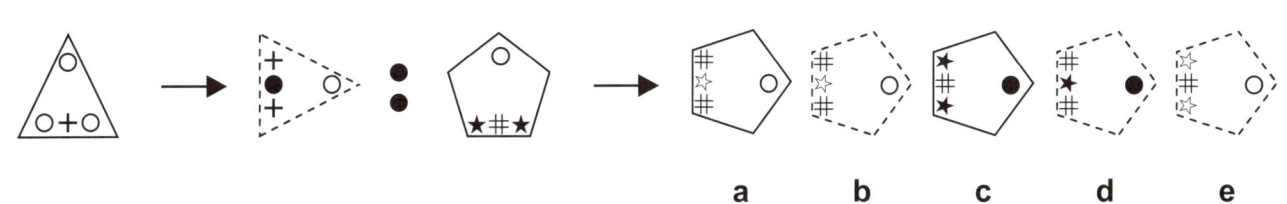

9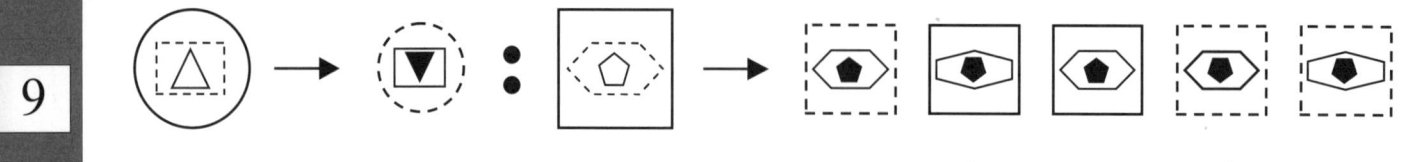

10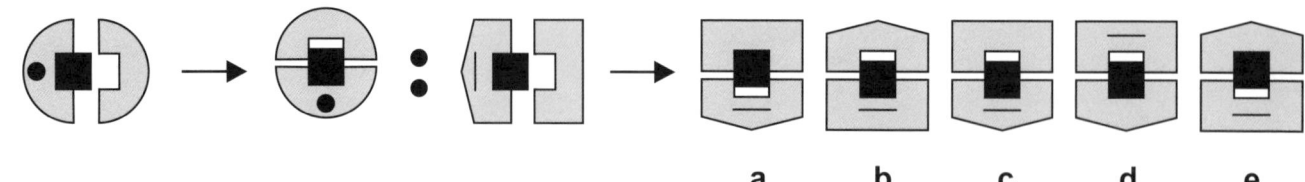

11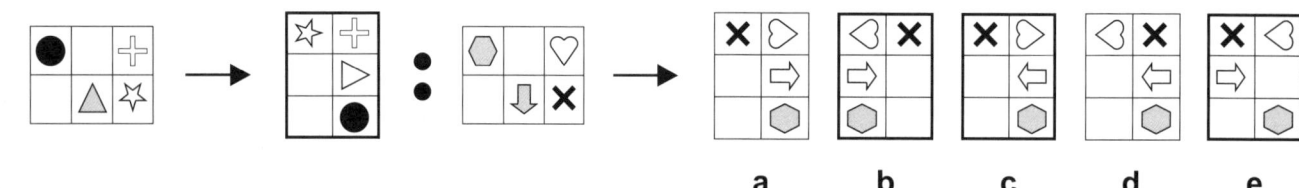

12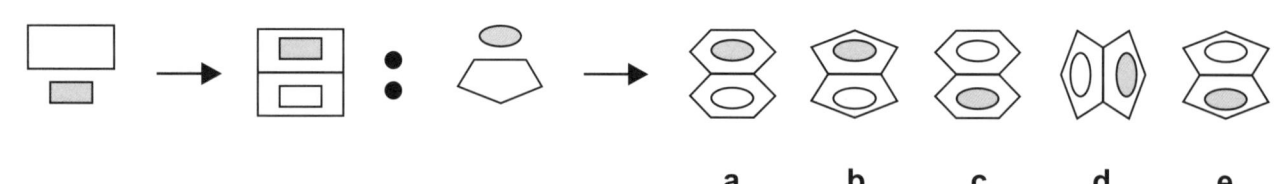

MOVE ON TO THE NEXT SECTION

Section D

In the following questions there are two shapes on the left-hand side that are similar in some way. On the right-hand side there are five other shapes.

You must decide which **one** of the five shapes is most like the pair on the left side of the page. Circle the letter under the shape, or mark the appropriate box on the multiple choice answer sheet.

Example

a b c d e

Answer: a

1

a b c d e

2

a b c d e

3

a b c d e

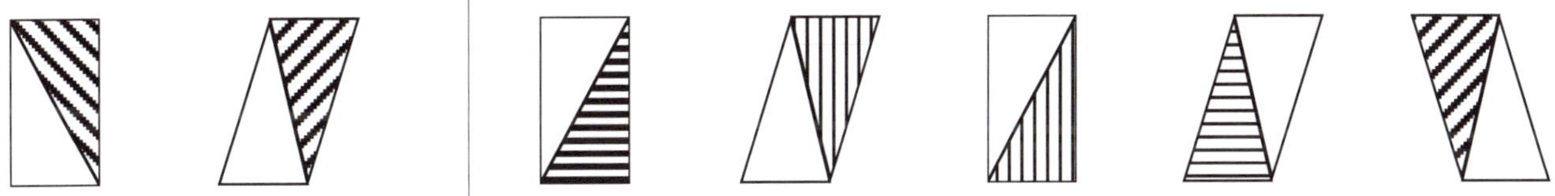

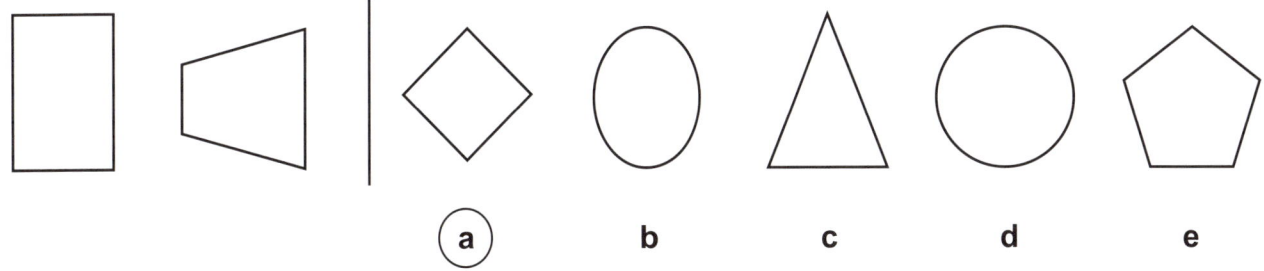

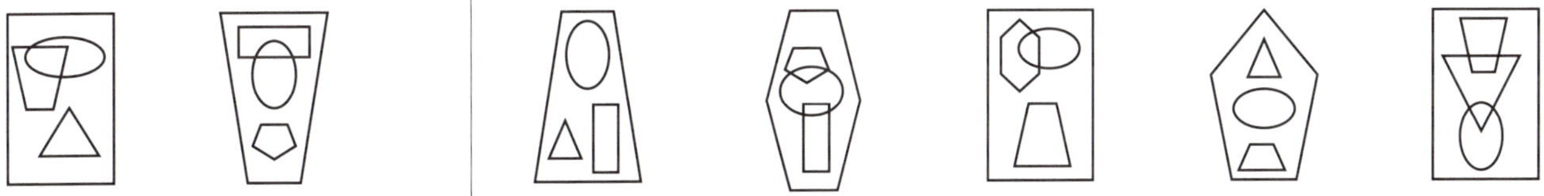

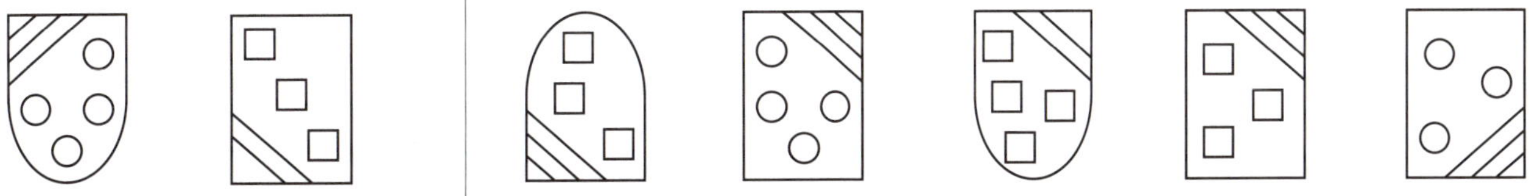

MOVE ON TO THE NEXT PAGE

4

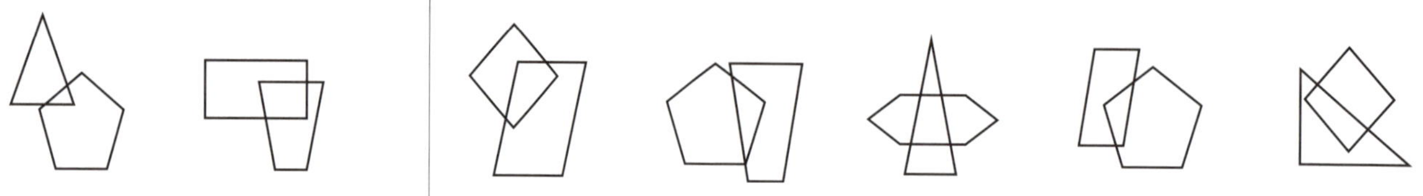

a b c d e

5

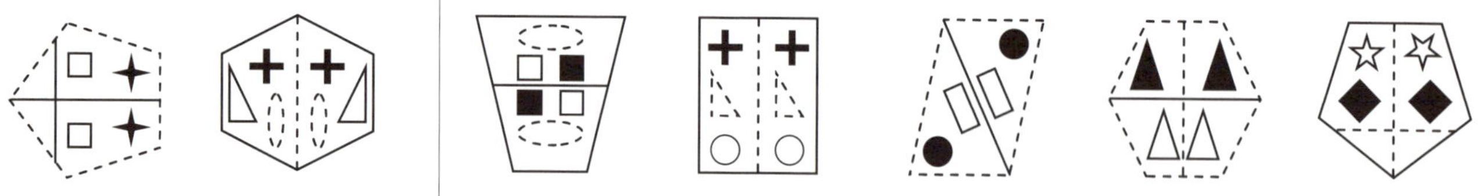

a b c d e

6

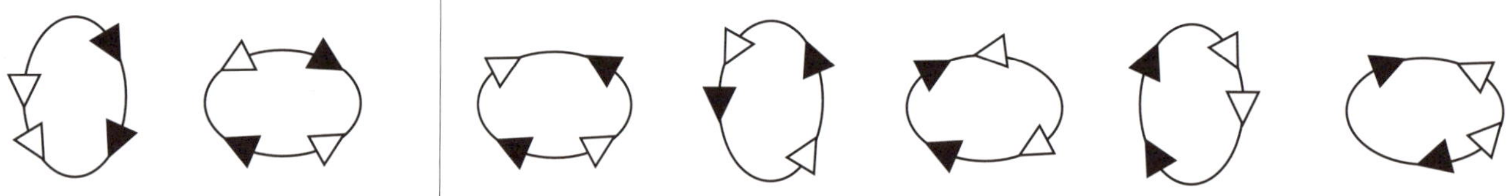

a b c d e

7

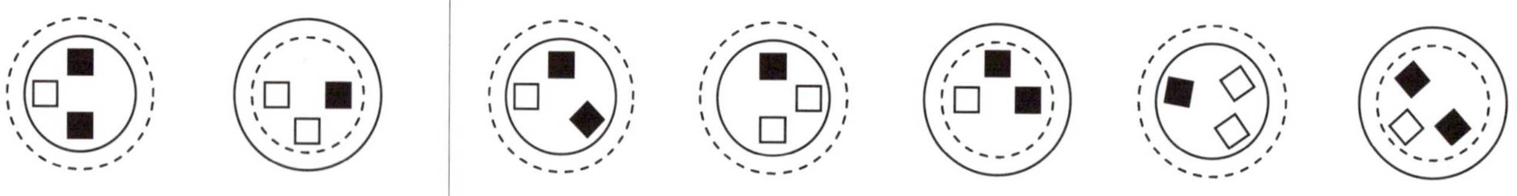

a b c d e

8

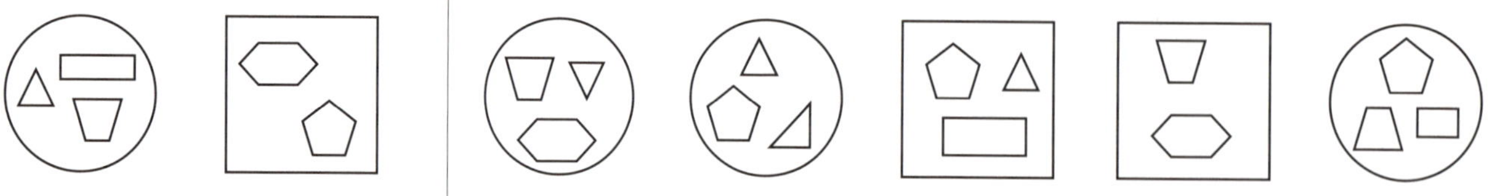

a b c d e

9

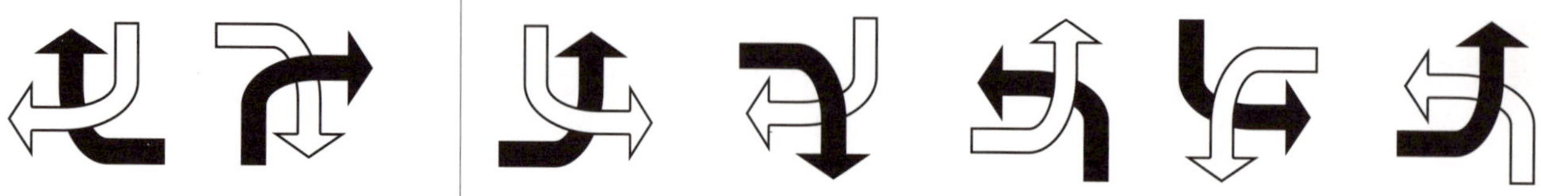

a b c d e

MOVE ON TO THE NEXT PAGE

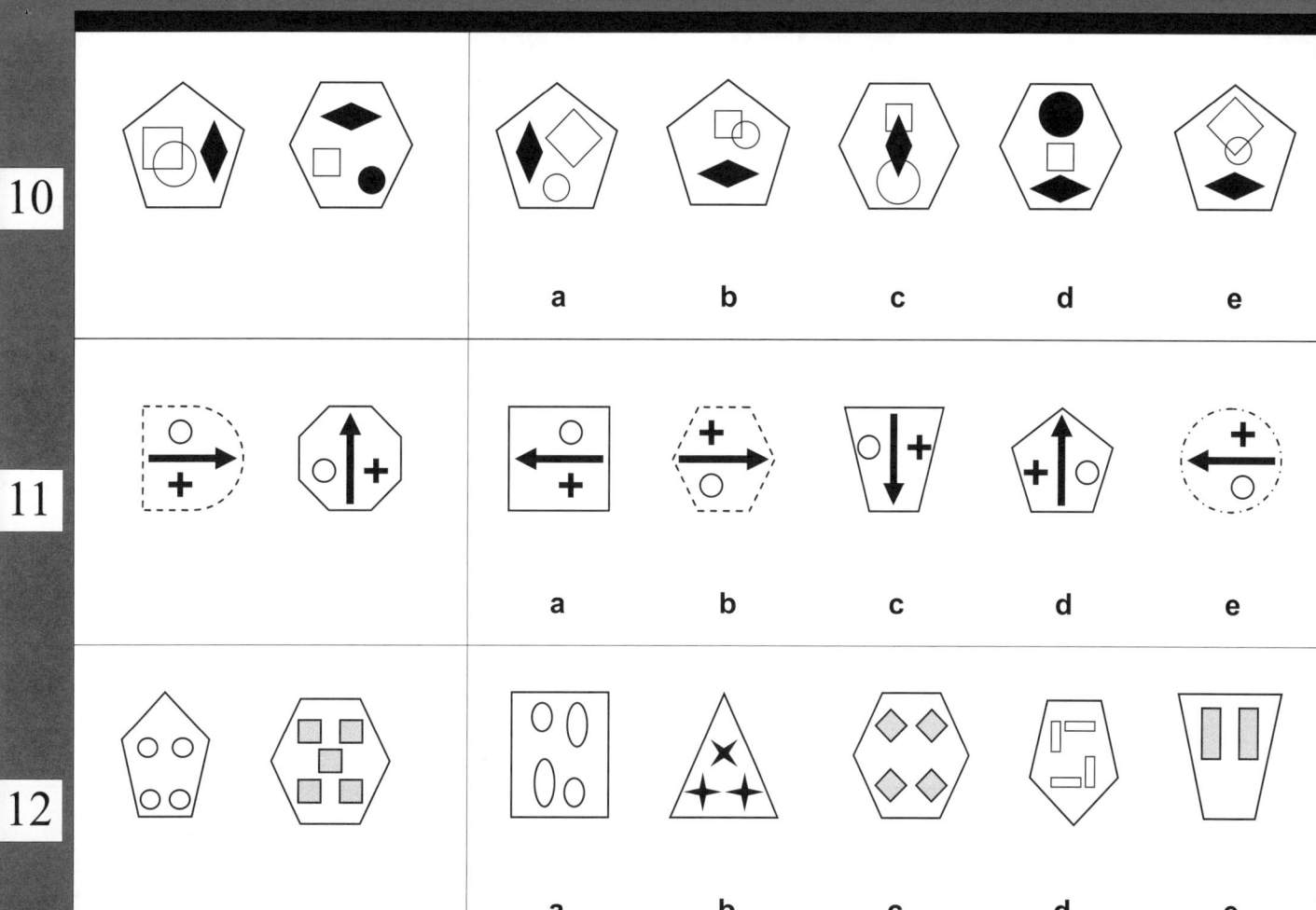

Section E

In the following questions there is a large square made up of smaller ones.
One of the smaller squares has been left blank.

You must choose one of the boxes from the right hand side that will take the place of the empty box and complete the pattern. Circle the letter below it, or mark the appropriate box on the multiple choice answer sheet.

Example

 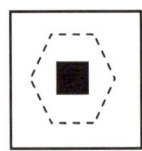 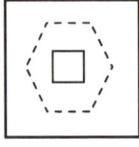   

                                        a   b   c   e

Answer: d

1

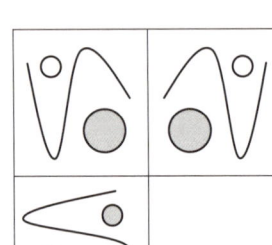 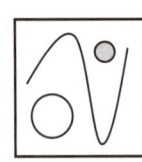 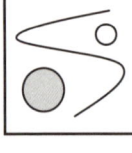   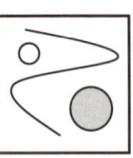

                                        a   b   c   d   e

2

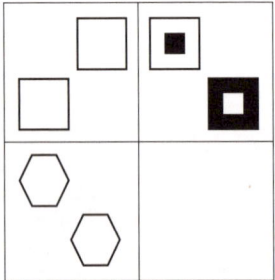 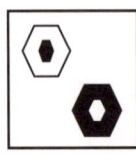 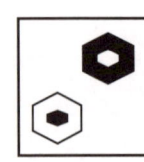 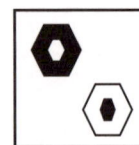 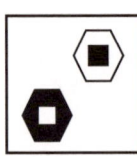 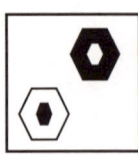

                                        a   b   c   d   e

MOVE ON TO THE NEXT PAGE

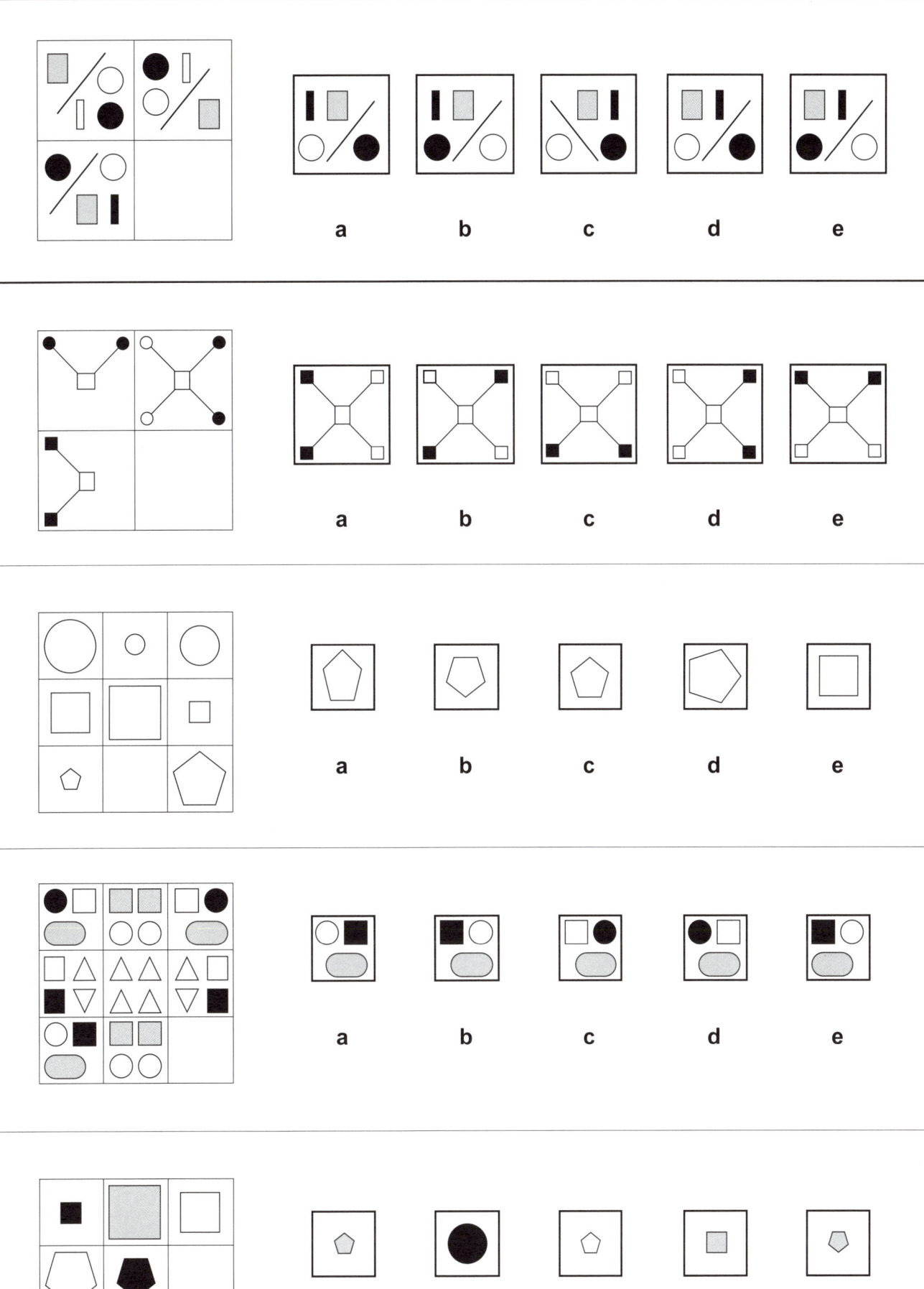

YOU ARE AT THE END OF THE TEST